The Tree of the Knowledge of Good and Evil Has Complex Roots
– "Ye Cannot Serve both God and Mammon" (Matthew 6:24)

The Money Tree

GOOD & EVIL ROOTS

1Timothy 6:10

For the love of money is the root of all evil: which while some coveted after, they have erred from the faith, and pierced themselves through with many sorrows

By Pastor Thornton Bell, Sr.

The Money Tree

Good and Evil Roots

Published By:

Thornton Bell - IMPACT NOW Ministries

For more information or to order additional books, please write:
Thornton Bell – IMPACT NOW Ministries
P. O. Box 1354
Birmingham, Alabama 35201
Phone (205) 655-6708

www.lulu.com/papasseafood

tmbell2@hotmail.com

Edited By: Thornton Bell

ISBN 978-0-6151-5183-0

Printed in the United States of America

Table of Contents

"ToT"

Missed forever,

My mother,

Annie Mae Bell

Money is eating away at the core of our Christian, moral and American values. It seems that many are succumbing to the money trap. The poor gets poorer while the rich gets greedier. Both ends lead to the love of money. You cannot serve both God and money. The love of money is the root of all evil. God's Word provides an answer.

This is the core of the message presented by Pastor Thornton Bell in his thoughtful treatise, The Money Tree – Good and Evil Roots. Using current events, biblical history and specific scripture, Pastor Bell explains the dilemma facing America and some of today's biggest churches. He challenges us to make changes in the attitudes, behavior, faith, and beliefs of society today.

Concise, thoughtful and factual, The Money Tree – Good and Evil Roots is an inspirational work for people of all faiths as they walk with God.

DAB

Consumers or consumed?

Humans are amazing creatures. We become extensions of what we eat. We think we are devouring it but it actually consumes us. For instance, since our arrival as babies, we have been consuming food. We were made to eat and if we stop eating, we wither away and die. We must take in food, oxygen, and water to sustain our physical bodies. God made us this way and we cannot change it. Likewise, if we absorb more than we need, we can expect some negative consequence to our bodies. Too much sugar causes diabetes to consume us. Too much salt causes high blood pressure to consume us. Smoking causes cancer to consume us. Breathing air is vital for life but too much or too little oxygen at

PRELUDE

particular air pressures will kill us. The right amount of water is good for us but too little dehydrates us and too much drowns us.

For some unknown reason, the process works the same way with our spirit, mind, body, and soul. Our life constantly absorbs in all dimensions and by design, what we take into our spirit, mind, body, and soul describes us. Jesus said, "Man cannot live by bread alone, but by every word that proceed out of the mouth of God". If we eat the word of God, it will begin to absorb us. As you will see, this is a good thing. Be serious about what you eat. Eat right and you will become right. Jesus spoke the following about the Word of God consuming us when he said the following:

John 15:7
If ye **abide** in me, and my **words abide** in you, ye shall ask what ye will, and it shall be done unto you.

Pastor Thornton Bell, Sr.

Forward

Most of what we consume comes from others. We arrived on earth depending on our mother's milk and nurturing. Anyone can see that since then, we have depended on someone other than ourselves for the necessities of life - our clothing, our water, our heat, our car, and our houses, etc... The list goes on. Humanity's production and supply system is intricately intertwined. No one can make it alone. We need others to produce most of the stuff that we require. Fortunately, people have devised a scheme for obtaining necessities. In our society, we purchase life necessities with MONEY.

Money can be a blessing or a challenge to our faith. Having wealth, (an abundance of money) presents a subtle temptation to our real faith in God. Underneath wealth is a dependency, which opens the door to fear and greed. On the other hand, poverty (a shortage of money) comes with serious problems too. Inside poverty is a dangerous illusion about money, which breeds covetousness. In each case, the core adversary is the "love of money".

One thing thou lackest.

In spite of all you have and all that you do, are you lacking one more important thing? Are you willing to sell everything, give to the poor, and follow Jesus? This book looks at the inherent implications of poverty, wealth, and faith. Most of the book is based on the spirit of the following scripture.

Mark 10:

17   And when he was gone forth into the way, there came one running, and kneeled to him, and asked him, Good Master, what shall I do that I may inherit eternal life?

18   And Jesus said unto him, Why callest thou me good? there is none good but one, that is, God.

19   Thou knowest the commandments, Do not commit adultery, Do not kill, Do not steal, Do not bear false witness, Defraud not, Honour thy father and mother.

20   And he answered and said unto him, Master, all these have I observed from my youth.

21   Then Jesus beholding him loved him, and said unto him, **One thing thou lackest**: go thy way, sell whatsoever thou hast, and give to the poor, and thou shalt have treasure in heaven: and come, take up the cross, and follow me.

22   And he was sad at that saying, and went away grieved: for he had great possessions.

23   And Jesus looked round about, and saith unto his disciples, How hardly shall they that have riches enter into the kingdom of God!

24   And the disciples were astonished at his words.   But Jesus answereth again, and saith unto them, Children, how hard is it for them that trust in riches to enter into the kingdom of God!

25   It is easier for a camel to go through the eye of a needle, than for a rich man to enter into the kingdom of God.

26   And they were astonished out of measure, saying among themselves, Who then can be saved?

27   And Jesus looking upon them saith, With men it is
     impossible, but not with God: for with God all things
     are possible.

Pulling camels through the eye of a needle

Remember when Jesus overturned the tables and scourged the crooks in
the temple. The bible says that his disciples reacted in the following
manner when he threw the moneychangers and those that sold goods out
of the temple.

> **John 2:17 -** And his disciples remembered that it was written,
> ***The zeal of thine house hath eaten me up.***

I can understand why some might ask the following questions:

- *What were the disciples truly thinking?*

- *What was so bad about the "Moneychangers"?*

- *Are churches returning to the problem?*

- *Are the cares of this world and the zeal for money eating away again at
  the houses of prayer?*

What began as a simple look at how some of the richest Americans
influence the world unveils immense concern. This is an important and
complex subject.   Notwithstanding, I am obligated to disclose the
impious ramifications of greed on this world and attempt to suggest a
biblical perspective for changing the trend.

Coincidentally, the year of 2006 revealed alarming exploits of money and
power. The rich and powerful are at work in issues ranging from rising

health costs, "big oil's" war pressures, and gasoline hikes, to biased networks' news propaganda. Like wild locusts, they swarm causing a range of critical consequences cloaked in camaraderie, inequities, charities, disagreements, disputes, minor skirmishes, all out wars, and worldwide catastrophe. Yet, in all these things, somehow the rich manages to keep on getting richer.

As the world's riches nation, the United States of America has much on which to reflect. "Respected" America is losing power to its greedy way with money. Many of the very wealthy are simply creating hysteria in some parts of the world in their quest for more riches. From China to Zimbabwe, the old ways of lives are changing. Increasingly, money's complex allusions are making it difficult to find untainted refuges in our world. Nevertheless, as difficult as it may be, we can find peace right in front of our faces. We can thank God for the unchanging shelter - His Word. In spite of it all, God gives us real sobering instructions about the consequences of riches.

The problem started in the Garden of Eden. In Eden, were sown new seeds of affection called **_lust_** and **_desire_**[1]. This deceiving taste for something extra goaded Eve into taking a forbidden fruit from a forbidden tree.

Good and Evil Roots
Obviously, a tree capable of producing two opposite fruits; namely _good_ and _evil_ requires comparable roots; namely good and evil. Moreover, the

---

[1] **1 John 2:16** For all that is in the world, the lust of the flesh, and the lust of the eyes, and the pride of life, is not of the Father, but is of the world

fruit of that tree should also yield seeds, which are capable of producing similar fruit. The phenomenon of seed is fascination to consider. Just think. Each of us began our lives on earth as a seed. What is even more mind boggling is that each of us can be biblically traced back to the seed of Noah[2] and ultimately back to Adam[3].

How often have you heard he phrase "you are what you eat"? Both, Adam and Eve ate and assumedly digested the forbidden fruit. Thus, this forbidden substance assimilated and manifested itself in their flesh, attitude, and their spirit. Each of us knows that what we take into our bodies has an affect on us. Even small portions of chemicals can affect our flesh, attitude, and spirit. Just ask any alcoholic or drug addict today. Likewise, our affection for and stewardship of money reveals the state of our flesh, attitude, and spirit[4]. That state is a function of what we take into our spirits.

Surely, the effects of the forbidden fruit consumed by Adam and Eve are evident in humanity today. This forbidden fruit produced the first recorded dispute between people. Can you imagine? With only four documented people existing on earth, a fight broke out. Furthermore, the dispute was between two brothers. The problem: what should God accept in exchange for His favor? What was Cain thinking? Can you imagine someone believing that he had a right to determine what God should like or dislike? In other words, imagine someone telling God;

---

[2] **Genesis 9:19** These are the three sons of Noah: and of them **was the whole earth overspread.**

[3] **Genesis 4:25** And Adam knew his wife again; and she bare a son, and called his name Seth: For God, said she, hath appointed me another **seed** instead of Abel, whom Cain slew.

[4] **Matthew 6:21** For where your **treasure** is, there will your **heart** be also.

"my fruit is worth more than his sheep". "God, his offering to you is not good enough". In addition to his obvious poor understanding of God, Cain did not realize another key principle. Namely, the recipient sets the value when they own everything anyway. Thus, began the perpetual argument over what should be the appropriate medium of exchange for goods and services. We specifically ask; what is a proper standard for determining *value*? By the way, let us call it *"money"*.

Money: Good Roots, Good Fruit

Or

Evil Roots, Evil Fruit

Here is a good news bad news story. The good news is money. The bad news is also money. Money is a necessity in this modern world. Then again, at a relative point, having too little or too much is problematic. Following are sample scriptural references that discuss man's dilemma with money:

- ## Money comes from God

  Ecclesiastes 5:19
  Every man also to whom God hath given riches and wealth, and hath given him power to eat thereof, and to take his portion, and to rejoice in his labour; this is the gift of God.

- ## Understanding the true source of money

  Deuteronomy 8:18
  But thou shalt remember the LORD thy God: for it is he that

giveth thee power to get wealth, that he may establish his covenant which he sware unto thy fathers, as it is this day

- **Having money is better than poverty**

Proverbs 10:15

The rich man's wealth is his strong city: the destruction of the poor is their poverty.

- **Money is necessary**

Ecclesiastes 7:12

For wisdom is a defence, and money is a defence: but the excellency of knowledge is, that wisdom giveth life to them that have it.

Ecclesiastes 10:19

A feast is made for laughter, and wine maketh merry: but money answereth all things

- **Lending with interest is bad.**

Exodus 22:25

If thou lend money to any of my people that is poor by thee, thou shalt not be to him as an usurer, neither shalt thou lay upon him usury.

- **Lend without interest**

Psalm 15:5

He that putteth not out his money to usury, nor taketh

reward against the innocent. He that doeth these things shall never be moved.

• Money cannot buy salvation

<u>Isaiah 55:1</u>

Ho, every one that thirsteth, come ye to the waters, and he that hath no money; come ye, buy, and eat; yea, come, buy wine and milk without money and without price.

• Money cannot buy Holiness

<u>Acts 8:20</u>

But Peter said unto him, Thy money perish with thee, because thou hast thought that the gift of God may be purchased with money.

• Salvation is difficult for the rich but possible

<u>Matthew 19</u>

23)   Then said Jesus unto his disciples, Verily I say unto you, That a rich man shall hardly enter into the kingdom of heaven.

24)   And again, I say unto you, It is easier for a camel to go through the eye of a needle, than for a rich man to enter into the kingdom of God.

25)   When his disciples heard it, they were exceedingly amazed, saying, Who then can be saved?

26)   But Jesus beheld them, and said unto them, With men this is impossible; but with God all things are possible.

- ## **Money is a false foundation**

  Proverbs 28:11
  The rich man is wise in his own conceit; but the poor that hath understanding searcheth him out.

- ## **Money is not permanent**

  Ecclesiastes 6:2
  A man to whom God hath given riches, wealth, and honour, so that he wanteth nothing for his soul of all that he desireth, yet God giveth him not power to eat thereof, but a stranger eateth it: this is vanity, and it is an evil disease.

- ## **Be careful when boasting about money**

  Psalms 49:

  5)   Wherefore should I fear in the days of evil, when the iniquity of my heels shall compass me about?

  6)   They that trust in their wealth, and boast themselves in the multitude of their riches;

  7)   None of them can by any means redeem his brother, nor give to God a ransom for him:

<u>Psalm 49:10</u>

For he seeth that wise men die, likewise the fool and the brutish person perish, and leave their wealth to others.

- **Money cannot to be trusted**

<u>Psalm 52:7</u>

Lo, this is the man that made not God his strength; but trusted in the abundance of his riches, and strengthened himself in his wickedness.

- **Money is a ruthless tempter**

<u>Proverbs 28:20</u>

A faithful man shall abound with blessings: but he that maketh haste to be rich shall not be innocent.

- **Beware of dangerous nobility**

<u>Jeremiah 9:23</u>

Thus saith the LORD, Let not the wise man glory in his wisdom, neither let the mighty man glory in his might, let not the rich man glory in his riches:

- **Beware of dangerous self gratification**

<u>Deuteronomy 8:17</u>

And thou say in thine heart, My power and the might of mine hand hath gotten me this wealth.

<u>2 Chronicles 1:11</u>

And God said to Solomon, Because this was in thine heart,

and thou hast not asked riches, wealth, or honour, nor the life of thine enemies, neither yet hast asked long life; but hast asked wisdom and knowledge for thyself, that thou mayest judge my people, over whom I have made thee king:

2 Chronicles 1:12
Wisdom and knowledge is granted unto thee; and I will give thee riches, and wealth, and honour, such as none of the kings have had that have been before thee, neither shall there any after thee have the like.

Proverbs 13:11
Wealth gotten by vanity shall be diminished: but he that gathereth by labour shall increase.

Proverbs 13:22
A good man leaveth an inheritance to his children's children: and the wealth of the sinner is laid up for the just.

- **Money brings false comfort**

  Proverbs 18:11
  The rich man's wealth is his strong city, and as an high wall in his own conceit.

- **Money breeds insomnia**

  Ecclesiastes 5:12
  The sleep of a labouring man is sweet, whether he eat little or much: but the abundance of the rich will not suffer him to sleep.

- ## The love trap - Money

  <u>1 Timothy 6:10</u>

  For the love of money is the root of all evil: which while some coveted after, they have erred from the faith, and pierced themselves through with many sorrows.

- ## Money can be deceitful

  <u>Matthew 13:22</u>

  He also that received seed among the thorns is he that heareth the word; and the care of this world, and the deceitfulness of riches, choke the word, and he becometh unfruitful.

  <u>Mark 4:19</u>

  And the cares of this world, and the deceitfulness of riches, and the lusts of other things entering in, choke the word, and it becometh unfruitful.

Having money brings benefits but one must not put too much faith in it. The book of Hebrews tells us that the difference between Cain and Abel was in their faith in God[5]. Without faith, it is impossible to please God.

.

---

[5] **Hebrews 11:4** By faith Abel offered unto God a more excellent sacrifice than Cain, by which he obtained witness that he was righteous, God testifying of his gifts: and by it he being dead yet speaketh.

Prelude

My Country, 'Tis of Thee

> *"America," is an American patriotic song. The melody is derived from the British national anthem, "God Save the Queen".*
>
> *The lyrics to "My Country, 'Tis of Thee" were written in 1831 by Reverend Samuel Francis Smith of Boston's Park Street Church while at the Andover Theological Seminary in Andover, Massachusetts. The song served as a de facto national anthem for much of the 19th century.*

I learned this song as a child while in kindergarten. I guess we heard it so much in the classroom and on the radio until the words just stuck in my memory. You see, World War 2 was underway and children who lived in the projects were taught spiritual and patriotic songs. It was commonly expected of us since our families were given decent housing subsidies by the government. I took it all to heart. In my heart, I loved my country and I loved my God. In my mind, I was a true American. When Kate Smith sung "God Bless America", I tried my best to out sing her each time I heard it. Yes, this was **my** country from the ocean, to the prairie, to the mountains white with snow. When I would sing those words *"God bless America, my homes sweet home"*, I knew God would do just that.

I was more than just a patriot. I cherished my country. Being poor did not bother me. Living in the projects did not bother me. Some things were disappointing, like being called "colored", riding in the back of the bus, having to eat outside at restaurants, having to drink from broken down water facets that were marked "colored", having to attend second rate segregated schools in Birmingham, Alabama or seeing my mother leave home to clean and iron for white people. Nevertheless, none affected my patriotism. This was my country and it could do no wrong. I made my pledge of allegiance to the flag each morning at kindergarten and pledged it again when I returned home.

I was naively convinced that this was God's way. Rich people were supposed to be rich Americans. We Blacks were meant to be poor Americans but we were still all Americans. We were a united country and we all cared about each other regardless of race because this was America.

Verse 1

> My country, 'tis of thee,
>
> Sweet land of liberty,
>
> Of thee I sing;
>
> Land where my fathers died,
>
> Land of the pilgrims' pride,
>
> From every mountainside
>
> Let freedom ring!

Verse 2

> My native country, thee,
>
> Land of the noble free,
>
> Thy name I love;

I love thy rocks and rills,

Thy woods and templed hills;

My heart with rapture thrills,

Like that above.

Verse 3

Let music swell the breeze,

And ring from all the trees

Sweet freedom's song;

Let mortal tongues awake;

Let all that breathe partake;

Let rocks their silence break,

The sound prolong.

Verse 4

My father's God to Thee,

Author of liberty,

To Thee we sing.

Long may our land be bright,

With freedom's holy light,

Protect us by Thy might,

Great God our King.

Verse 5 *(added to celebrate Washington's Centennial)*

Our joyful hearts today,

Their grateful tribute pay,

Happy and free,

After our toils and fears,

After our blood and tears,

Strong with our hundred years,

God, to Thee.

My country 'Tis of Thee

"Tis of Thee" speaks about a nation dedicated to God. Hence, I could think of no better place to start this book than at the biblical beginning of humanity. I mean - at the true beginning. Let us say, the place where God first made man. You see, after the first "very good"[6] six days of God's creation, something began to go wrong.

> **Genesis 2:17**
>
> But of the tree of the knowledge of good and evil, thou shalt not eat of it: for in the day that thou eatest thereof thou shalt surely die.

One interesting point is that God spoke about an impending problem even before Adam or Eve had eaten of the fruit of the tree that contained the knowledge of good and evil. After giving Adam instructions concerning the tree, God said, "it is not good for man to be alone". Could it be that the maker of both the tree and the man knew the alluringly predetermined effects from placing a forbidden fruit in the garden within the grasp of man? Perhaps, man's taste for the fruit was intentionally placed there by God. Surely, it was God that made man and man did not make himself. Obviously, whatever man was capable of doing came from God. The answer rests in a key attributes that makes us the image and likeness of God. This characteristic is our ability to make and own our choices. Freedom of **choice** is one of the most

---

[6] **Genesis 1:31** And God saw every thing that he had made, and, behold, it was **very good**. And the evening and the morning were the sixth day.

My Country 'Tis of Thee

important attributes of people but in order for it to qualify as a true choice; one must own the corresponding consequences.

The Roots of the forbidden Tree

According to the bible, after God made man, He planted a garden in a place called Eden. Moreover, He placed the man who He had made in the garden. This garden had food that was both good looking and good tasting. However, God declared one of the trees as forbidden and deadly to people. Unfortunately, without knowing good and evil, the man had no real understanding about death. Having the ability to make choices without knowledge and understanding is a recipe for disastrous consequences.

What a dilemma. What is it about us that make us so naturally curious? The woman, who was later called Eve, just had to ask the questions. Ah ha! What is it that God is trying to keep from me? What is so special about that particular tree anyway? What is wrong with a little taste of the knowledge of good and evil? We humans must always push the envelope and see for ourselves. What an irony. We must taste what is "eating at" us.

Now, I know that at my weight, I should never eat more than one small slice of apple pie for dinner. However, I also know that when dinner is over, my appetite stirs me to the point that I can hear apple pie calling me from the refrigerator - even in my dreams.

Thus, the scene was set in the Garden of Eden. Disobedience became inevitable. Moreover, a subtle tempter was lurking. The *tempter* understood from experience that at the root of the tree was the love of the power that accompanies ultimate wealth or rather the "love of money". I know, you are asking, why the love of money? For the love of money **is** "the root of all evil".

Please notice "ALL EVIL". You see, money is not just the means or standard for facilitating the exchange of goods. Something must also be given up in exchange for it. The more you use it, the more you must give up. Over the years, I have noticed that the more money I gain, the more I will be required to give up in getting it. Money is power. This world grants godly reverence and power to those who possess excessive amounts of it. However, misplaced power drains us and leaves this world empty handed.

A subtle tempter was also there to make things more difficult. This was the greatest "Bling Bling" of all times. Not only did he have money, he was the "stuff". His glitter was designed to advertise money and power. He was both the music and the bright lights in a walking commercial for lust and desire. Just look at the way Ezekiel describes him.

Ezekiel 28:13

Thou hast been in Eden the garden of God; every precious stone was thy covering, the sardius, topaz, and the diamond, the beryl, the onyx, and the jasper, the sapphire, the emerald, and the carbuncle, and gold: the workmanship of thy tabrets and of thy pipes was prepared in thee in the day that thou wast created.

It is hard to be friends with someone who has a great deal of money - especially when you do not have any yourself. You wonder if they think they are better than you are. They wonder if you are their friend just for the money. No doubt, the woman of the Garden of Eden had already become bored with the man's wisdom as she thought; "hmm, I need more. Now what would it be like to be as wise as God". Notice how Adam (the man) never actually sought after wisdom. He just took the fruit from his wife and ate it. The ambiance of greed tends to siphon those who are in the vicinity.

> ### Genesis 3:6
> And when the woman saw that the tree was good for food,
> and that it was pleasant to the eyes, and a tree to be desired
> to make one wise, she took of the fruit thereof, and did eat,
> and gave also unto her husband with her; and he did eat.

Desire and fear are precursors for the pursuit of money. For many, at a point, worldly desire compromises the essence of our moral fiber - the inner soul. For some, fear compels us to gather in excess now to forego a future unforeseen lack. Somehow, we think we can predict our future. Jesus asked us, "What would we give in exchange for our soul"[7]. Desire puts an unquenchable hunger in our souls.

"It's the economy stupid". I remember that slogan winning an election for one of the most morally deficient presidents of my time. For many Americans, some of these notions are hard to grasp and even more difficult to accept. Our inner psychic has been numbed by contrary propaganda. From birth, we have been indoctrinated by a controlling,

---

[7] **Matthew 16:26** For what is a man profited, if he shall gain the whole world, and lose his own soul? or what shall a man give in exchange for his soul?

My Country 'Tis of Thee

compelling, and even hypnotic trance called "capitalism". This force works in our subconscious. If unchecked, it captivates and overcomes our innocence.

Did it say "In God We Trust"?

Capitalism = Seizing The Moment

Capitalism in its raw form is defined as "an economic system wherein the means of production are mostly privately owned, and capital is invested in the production, distribution and other trade of goods and services, for profit"[8]. According to Webster's Third New International Dictionary, the root word, capital, derives from the Latin word "capitalis", which ultimately comes from caput, meaning, "head".

Consequently, intrinsic in our capitalistic society is a desire to become the head or as we say it "get ahead". Unfortunately, the method for getting ahead means gaining even more value with each transaction or

---

[8] Wikepedia The Free Encyclopedia

My Country 'Tis of Thee

exchange. This is called "profiting". Our intuitions authorize us to exploit each transaction. Consequently, items that start with a value of $10 may ultimately reach a value of $1,000. Any missed profit in a transaction is deemed a lost opportunity or more commonly a "loss".

At the core of the capitalistic psychic is an acute sensitivity to the notion of "profit and losses". This sensitive dance breeds distrust or cautiousness during transactions between those that have and those who are trying to get. As a consequence, capitalism groups us into classes. Obviously, if one "gets ahead" another is left behind.

Capital also describes money. Eve had achieved all she could within her permitted boundaries within the Garden of Eden. Since Adam offered no new challenges, she sought more wisdom to compete with God. I can just hear her saying: "Adam, eat this fruit" and afterward "why are we standing here naked". Could that be why God said to Adam, "Because thou has hearkened to the voice of thy wife...?" Some of us are just pushed to pursue wealth while others are in ambitious pursuit.

On a personal note, I recently sold one of my used tenor saxophone mouthpieces on the web site called "Ebay.com". I paid about $325 for it about nine years ago but it sold at an auction price of $785. For about 12 hours after the sale, I was ecstatic about my profit until I saw one similar to mine which was of lesser quality selling for $1,500. For a moment, I felt disappointed and cheated until I finally realized the effects that society was having on my psychic. The $460 profit I had made on the item was enough until I saw what another person was

My Country 'Tis of Thee

making. I must be careful. This was borderline greed and covetousness. Capital is money. Capitalism is profiteering.

Left unchecked, our capitalistic attitude can bring out the worse in us. This becomes increasingly risky to humanity as technology hastens capitalism to spread globally. The current outcome is worldwide classifications based on wealth. It follows that capitalism spawns "categorization and classification". The categories are as follows: those who are *leaders* (heads), those who are *benefactors* (close to heads, like advisors or lawyers), those who *benefits* (spouse, children), those who are *beneficent* (just from being around), those who receive *benevolence* (charities), those who provide *benediction* (ceremonial relief through amusement), and those who are *beneath* (poverty - workers). In my America (my country tis of thee), we are classed according to our capital assets.

I think I was about five or six years old when I first realized that I was classified lower than some. My mother worked for some rich white people who had horses and a big house on the other side of town. I cherished her taking me with her occasionally to play with my little white friend and his pony. He had so many things with which to play. We had so much fun together. However, it ended one day when Miss Smith told my mother to stop me from playing with little Daniel. It must have been the way she said it that made my mother mad. I can still picture my mother; upset and saying "I am not working for that white lady again, ever". She never did either. Being black and poor, I could only dream of playing with horses and ponies after that. All the same, I

My Country 'Tis of Thee

learned to make my own horses from broom and mop handles. In my imagination, I had just as much fun. Those were the good old days.

Is your ladder of success placed against the wrong tree?

The true ladder of success starts with the bottom rung. One lays a foundation, which becomes a platform for another to reach higher. It is also supported by an infallible truth.

At 13, I began to wonder. Is this actually "**my** country tis of thee"? Truthfully, as I grew older, I could see my nation falling into a perpetual trap of corruption and greed. Money had obsessed our national psychic. "In God we trust" changed to "in cash or credit we trust". I knew that as a nation, we could not love both God and money. My gut told me that something drastic was about to happen if we did not change our course soon.

Place your Ladder Upon The Rock

By the time I left high school, I knew that our nation needed to change its instincts. A house (or nation) built upon sand instead of a rock will not withstand hard times. A nation with genuine love and care for fellow citizens **is** as a house built on a "rock". A rock describes a strong foundation. Straightforwardly, we as a nation must put aside some of our capitalistic instincts and become more charitable if we are to survive. How can the *United* States be so divided?

Even though I understood this concept at my young age, I also knew that some around me were far too cunning and clever to consider helping others without a profit. Furthermore, racism and prejudices were clouding the issues and obstructing our national decency. From my perspective, it became difficult to tell if I was being classified based on greed, capitalism or merely racism.

Then again, being both black and poor in the South added a little more weight to the class issue. All the same, I learned a valuable lesson. You cannot place all your faith in a nation ruled by men.

Sweet Land of Liberty

America - A Divided House

Wow, this *is* the land of opportunity for some. This year, I read an article from Forbes magazine that estimated the monetary wealth of the world's richest people[9]. The list ranked the nations wealthiest according to net worth. Forbes magazine should be commended for this great source of information. However, the article should not stop there. We need to follow the money and see the exact influence it is having on the future and present lives of the masses. While some are becoming extremely rich, many others are also becoming extremely poor. Resources are limited. When money flows into one place, it affects the lives of others. Enormous gains on one side means great losses on the other. Since the rich is getting richer, the poor must be getting poorer. Thus, to insure equality, we must constantly examine the following questions.

1. How can one man accumulate $55 billion by the time he reaches 50 years old?

2. Why do Sam Walton's widow and four children need a combined wealth of more than $102.5 billion?

---

[9] http://www.forbes.com/billionaires/ (Edited by Luisa Kroll and Allison Fass 03.09.06, 6:00 PM ET)

3. Moreover, if only 400 people in the U. S. account for $1.22 trillion of the nations capital, who actually controls the country's remaining 330 million people?

4. Finally, does the preamble to the U. S. Constitution's "of the people", "by the people" and "for the people" include poor people too?

Here is a simple fact. **Those who make the rules are "rulers"**. Given the mindset of the current rulers, how can this become a sweet land of liberty for all?

What I mean is that riches and wealth can be traced back to sweat from someone's poor brow. The fact that "money flows" implies that it started at one point and ended at another. Implications of this tricky outcome is often lost in the course of achieving wealth.

Pa Pa's Theory of Wealth:

Excess wealth = sweat + suffering + wars + chaos + poverty

For each dollar gained beyond a certain level, there is an easily forgotten imbalance that generates hurt, tragedy, and losses. The pain and suffering dwarfs the consequential benefits and value on society as a whole.

Money divides us. A house divided cannot stand. Money separates us into categories and classes. Often, people are finding it permissible to segregate based on economics. Poor people are grouped together and

Sweet Land of Liberty

steered into lesser neighborhoods. Likewise, the rich is separated into the plush neighborhoods and guarded from the poor. Consequently, some humans are over here and other humans are over there. It hurts to see that our efforts to break the barriers of racial segregation only led us to an even more brutal economic segregation. Fences between people breed mistrust. The needs on the rich side of the fence capture the national attention while those of the other side are forgotten. I know. I lived on the broken streets.

Many have discussed the dichotomy between those that have and do not have in our society. Nevertheless, its ramification is becoming increasingly global in its scope. Countries are now grouped into categories called *First World*, *Second World* and *Third World* where the latter is now considered the workforce society that generates wealth for the rich. Cheap labor is now an acceptable norm. Something in my gut seems to know it is wrong for the president of the United States to say, "we are allowing them to work here because Americans won't do the job". What he truly means is that rich business owners can now make even more profits because labor is going to be cheaper.

Interestingly, even the devils of the Holy Bible are smart enough to understand the value of unity. Devils are united and do not fight one another. Devils also understand that humans' inner desire and greed will often lead us to warfare and even murder. Certainly, we see wars between people while our real enemy, the devil, remains steadfast and diligent in his attack against us. Jesus spoke the following:

Sweet Land of Liberty

Luke 11:18

If Satan also be divided against himself, how shall his kingdom stand? because ye say that I cast out devils through Beelzebub.

Matthew 12:25

And Jesus knew their thoughts, and said unto them, Every kingdom divided against itself is brought to desolation; and every city or house divided against itself shall not stand:

This dilemma places enormous pressure on those who have been fortunate enough to be called "rich". Wealth becomes fickle when the masses are uneasy. As the book title suggest, man cannot serve both God and Mammon.

Is mammon money?

Is mammon money? Alternatively, does money only become mammon when the riches of this world began to be loved? In that case, then how do we know when we have reached that threshold called *"greed* and *love of money"*?

This book endeavors to examine the limits of the mammon. The cornerstone premise is based on the following scriptures.

1 Timothy 6:10

For the love of money is the root of all evil: which while

some coveted after, they have erred from the faith, and pierced themselves through with many sorrows.

Matthew 6:24

No man can serve two masters: for either he will hate the one, and love the other; or else he will hold to the one, and despise the other. Ye cannot serve God and mammon.

Luke 16:13

No servant can serve two masters: for either he will hate the one, and love the other; or else he will hold to the one, and despise the other. Ye cannot serve God and mammon.

Genesis 3:6

And when the woman saw that the tree was good for food, and that it was pleasant to the eyes, and a tree to be desired to make one wise, she took of the fruit thereof, and did eat, and gave also unto her husband with her; and he did eat

Here is an accepted fact. Sin began when humanity disobeyed God, lusted for more, took the fruit and ate of the tree that contained the knowledge of good and evil. Now what was so bad about eating of the tree that contained the knowledge of good and evil? I would suggest that at the root of the tree was the "DNA" of evil; the love of the things that come from what we have learned to call "money".

- Money is what money buys.

Sweet Land of Liberty

- It brings us things for our pleasure.

- It makes us appear wiser

- It makes us appear empowered

In essence, money brings us value. I mean, it enables us to obtain the things that make us feel more valuable. We are not truly after the money as much as the things and power that it allows us to possess.

Sweet Land of Liberty

"The Love of Money" Roots?

<u>Root</u> = Primary Cause Or Primary Source

I recently had an excruciating toothache. The pain was unbearable. Nothing could touch my mouth. I could not stand cold water, hot coffee, or even food. I wanted to remove every tooth in my mouth. You see, the filling in one of my teeth had fallen out. My trip to the dentist was a nervous one as usual but all he did was extract the root nerve. He called it a root canal. Immediately afterwards, it was as if nothing had ever happened. All pain was gone. The dentist had removed the root cause of the pain.

To escape the money trap we must avoid the root of the problem - the *LOVE* of it.

Money Defined?

Understanding a thing enables us to determine how to control its effect on us. Surely, by understanding cancer, we have prevented many casualties. Since money is of this earth, we should have dominion over it[10]. Let us continually seek to understand money.

A most common definition of money refers to its function as a medium of exchange. However, money's real purpose is to provide a token of exchange for something of value, e.g., a standard. Even today, it remains difficult to set a stable reference point for apportioning value.

---

[10] **Psalm 72:8** He shall have **dominion** also from sea to sea, and from the river unto the ends

Sweet Land of Liberty

Let us say, 10 pennies equal exactly two chickens. What happens when the chickens are scarce? What happens when pennies are scarce? If I get the chickens now and pay later, should I pay the value based on the day I bought them or based on the current value at payoff. Hence, money has this intriguing, relative, and constantly moving value scale. Even so, having a relatively standard medium of exchange is considered more practical than an alternative system. That system is called bartering, which is often inefficient because it requires traders to place an equaling value on two different things based on their mutual needs and desires. It is difficult to find someone with a green Cadillac who wants to exchange it for my purple Buick when I hate red Cadillacs.

Over time, humanity has used various schemes to find an appropriate exchange medium. The sticking point is that each party must agree on the standard to be used. For example, if you give me 10 of the things that we both will always value and I will give you my car. Each transacting party should be able to retrieve the predetermined standard value within a mutually agreed timeframe without concern that value will be lost. Our American dollar is usually stable but I have a Zimbabwean Dollar that was two cents American a few years back but has since fallen 100 fold. (for example, from .02 to .0002 of a dollar). A $5,000 (Zim) necklace selling in Zimbabwe only cost me one dollar.

Often missed is the fact that things purchased with money usually require the work of someone to make the product. Too often, we find "sweat shops" and "cheap labor" at the core of product development.

Sweet Land of Liberty

At the core of product, development is a working class. The ability to manipulate monetary standards plays a vital role in sustaining dominance over the working class. I suppose in the end, one person's drop of sweat is equal to another's drop of sweat. But there seems to be an inescapable temptation for greed and power when you watch someone else sweat on your behalf.

This does not change except for the subjective perception of man's power. Eventually, money becomes a catalytic dialog between those who sweat to produce it and those who are sweating to get it. Civilization becomes both a facilitator and a buffer of the flow of money from one to the other. This dance of exchange is often called "service". One becomes served and another becomes a server. No matter how good the advertisement, many never leave the server role. Having someone serve you based on your wealth gives one a sense of *power* over another. Ah, there is the magic word – *POWER*. Riches bring a sense of *power*.

Is this land of *liberty* a sweet one for all? Sometimes it taste like a bitter pill.

Of Thee I Sing

The Mammon Song?

Oh, how I long and desire to sing for my country again but how do I sing for mammon?

Matthew 6:24

No man can serve two masters: for either he will hate the one, and love the other; or else he will hold to the one, and despise the other. Ye cannot serve God and mammon.

Mammon

The etymology of the word mammon suggests its use as a word for *money*. In the end, it boils down to *riches* or *benefits*. Several versions of biblical scriptures emphasize the synonymous relationship between mammon, riches, wealth and money. The Amplified version of Luke 16:9-13 makes a strong case for linking the evil influences of wealth. Please see the following scripture.

LUKE 16:9-13 *(Amplified Bible)*

And I tell you, make friends for yourselves by means of unrighteous mammon (deceitful riches, money, possessions), so that when it fails, they [those you have favored] may receive and welcome you into the everlasting habitations (dwellings).

He who is faithful in a very little [thing] is faithful also in much, and he who is dishonest and unjust in a very little [thing] is dishonest and unjust also in much.

Therefore if you have not been faithful in the [case of] unrighteous mammon (deceitful riches, money, possessions), who will entrust to you the true riches?

And if you have not proved faithful in that which belongs to another [whether God or man], who will give you that which is your own [that is, the true riches]?

No servant is able to serve two masters; for either he will hate the one and love the other, or he will stand by and be devoted to the one and despise the other. You cannot serve God and mammon (riches, or anything in which you trust and on which you rely).

Most Americans learn to value money early in life. Even the very young can become entrepreneurs. The arrival of instant media entertainment such as the internet, TV, Cell Phones, DVD and Movies make its luring effects inescapably tempting at an early age.

Our youths are chasing the "bling bling". Children are being killed over tennis shoes and gold necklace chains. Kids are learning to love money

Of Thee I Sing

more than they love people. When children begin to act this recklessly, we can be sure that the problems are becoming severe.

Adults should act swiftly and correctly to affect a change. However, just the contrary is happening. Since the year 2000, I have seen businesses and even some so called "Churches" rushing to covet money under the guise of a subtle temptation called "Faith Based Initiative". What once offered a chance to help the poor is often seen as a new source of prosperity for the greedy.

Where is the purity in charity these days? When I was young we sang and played music and games for the pure "art" or pleasure of it and none could deny the fruits of our creativity. Our musical gifts and physical talents made room for us even in the mist of a hateful and bigoted South. Today, many are asking the following question. Is our quest for money changing our inner passion for pure artistic expression?

What shall a man give (or give up) in exchange for his soul? The love of money is siphoning away our inner passions. What songs have you sung lately and why were you singing? Did not your fathers teach you better? I believe we are moving away from the values and passions about which our fathers taught us to sing.

Land where my Father Died

Blood, Sweat, Money
Money Sources

How important are the methods by which riches are obtained? While a most common definition of money refers to its function as a medium of exchange, if it qualifies as money, it must also be a token of exchange for something of value. In other words, those who give it up must believe it is getting an equally proportionate value for the amount exchanged. Even today, it is difficult to set an arbitrary reference point. Say, 10 pennies equal exactly two chickens. What happens when the chickens are scarce? What happens when pennies are scarce? If I get the chickens now and pay later, should I pay the value based on the day I bought them or based on the current value at payoff. Hence, money has an intriguingly relative value scale. Even so, having a relatively standard medium of exchange is considered more reasonable and convenient than *bartering*.

Over the years, men have used various schemes to attempt to find an appropriate exchange medium. To be very fair, sweat should be the real medium of exchange. We need a more equitable way to reward the labor effort. Today, labor unions are losing the parity argument.

Sweat and Slavery

One of America's most shameful legacies is that of Slavery. Free Labor creates the rich class far faster than cheap labor. For centuries, our country thrived on the backs and sweat of the poorest of the poor. Some of that wealthy heritage accumulated during that time of slavery shape our nation today. One may argue for or against reparations but injustices cannot be denied.

Sadly, slave owners used religion to justify their greed for money.[13] Even certain scriptures were exploited for greed; power and control (please see the scriptural footnote referenced below). This posed even more danger to our nation's moral psychic. Because some issues linger, similar tactics are perpetrated on our society today. Some even spill over into the churches. Reconciliation for the sins of slavery must begin within the hearts of the saints of God. We must each continually ask ourselves, "Have I reconciled my differences with former slaves or slave owners?" Perhaps, some vestige of slavery exist in America's current illegal immigration dilemma. Both are driven by greed and profits at the expense of another's labor.

Debt - a new slave master

Another clever but divisive method used to exploit Americans today is called *debt*. Many are only one paycheck away from monetary ruin. Enormous personal debts burden many Americans. The supporting statistics are astonishing. The original idea was to provide a technique for exchanging goods or services when a buyer has nothing to exchange. In other words, a pseudo exchange was enacted to allow the buyer to collect the goods or service upfront and pay the seller or a third party

---

[13] **Ephesians 6:5** **Servants**, be obedient to them that are your **masters** according to the flesh, with fear and trembling, in singleness of your heart, as unto Christ; **Colossians 3:22** **Servants**, obey in all things your **masters** according to the flesh; not with eyeservice, as menpleasers; but in singleness of heart, fearing God; **1 Peter 2:18** **Servants**, be subject to your **masters** with all fear; not only to the good and gentle, but also to the froward.

Land Where My Father Died

lender later. The lender paid for the goods sold then collected from the buyer at a prearranged time or in small portions (installments) over a range of time. This practice usually means higher costs to the buyer with each transaction. One cost is the profit charged by the seller and another cost is the usury or interest charged by the lender. In a capitalistic society, poor buyers are kept in a perpetual cycle of poverty by paying for the *seller cost + seller profits + lender usury*. Thus, the poor's little money is devalued even more by debt. I have seen the effects of the addiction to debt and credit cards on the poor. Initial satisfaction from debt usually leaves the poor with more poverty.

> ### Proverbs 14:31
>
> He that oppresseth the **poor** reproacheth his Maker: but he that honoureth him hath mercy on the poor.
>
> ### Proverbs 22:7
>
> The rich ruleth over the poor, and the borrower is servant to the lender.

21st Century Slavery?

21st Century Slavery?

Another subtle creature has emerged today. Growing are the abuses by some who see church-going members as merchandise. As a believer, I think we must face this issue head on. I call this the dawn of "Mega Churches". While greed and covetousness may also exist in smaller churches, the opportunity for corruption is greater in mega churches because of the masses and proximity. All the same, if church members everywhere are not watchful, their debts will grow even more while so called tithe collectors become wealthier.

Land Where My Father Died

2 Peter 2:3

And through covetousness shall they with feigned words
make merchandise of you: whose judgment now of a long
time lingereth not, and their damnation slumbereth not.

Now before you start wondering if I have bitten into some anti-church
growth serum, let me explain my point. I am definitely not against the
growth of the Kingdom of God. First of all, God's church (the true
body of Christ) is holy, unblemished and incorruptible. However,
through greed and craftiness, counterfeits are creeping in and deceiving
many on behalf of church growth. Consequently, we see an explosion in
so-called church growth in the wake of rising family burdens and
distresses. To wit, divorce rates, sex related diseases, promiscuity, drug
additions, murders, suicides and other oppressive tactics of the devil are
increasing. Many are innocently seeking answers to their problems from
these mega organizations. Accordingly, support groups and ministries
are being established for the same devilish spirits that we were told by
Jesus to cast out of people[14]. Government subsidized "Faith Based
Initiatives" are replacing genuine benevolence with money hungry lies to
gain access to program grants. Simple acts of faith and compassion are
now becoming big business ventures. Do we truly want to go there?

Obediently, members are diligently serving their spiritual masters who
demand money in support of their "vision". Misguidedly, some
members use their contributions like the lottery in hopes of striking it

---

[14] **Mark 16:17** And these signs shall follow them that believe; In my **name** shall they **cast out
devils**; they shall speak with new tongues;

Land Where My Father Died

rich by being obedient to the church visionaries. As a consequence, many are incurring more debt in order to meet "church" demands. Tithes and offerings are scriptural, good and proper but it is becoming hard to find incorruptible collectors sent by God who are willing to insist on storing God's money to meet the members' unforeseen needs.

Where have you seen a bona fide "storehouse" lately?[15] Saints must not be afraid to ask questions about money. What is truly happening to the offerings, tithes and special collections? How is money being dispersed? How much is going into the storehouse to meet the future needs of the people? Church leaders must be willing to answer these questions openly and honestly. Leaders must not be afraid of indisputable accountability. The members must be kept informed. Doing otherwise opens the door to the subtle trap of serving money in place of God.

Lately, I have noticed that many are quick to entertain insolent questions about God but are reluctant to question church leaders about money. Many givers have been convinced that questioning church finances somehow lessens the giver's faith in God's Word. To some, curiosity is a sign of rebellion. However, the fear of asking questions about money elevates money to an unmerited higher sacred level. Likewise, fearing the loss of blessings from God because questions are asked about money is a bit disingenuous. We must place less faith in money and men and more faith in the power of God.

---

[15] **Malachi 3:10** Bring ye all the tithes into the **storehouse**, that there may be meat in mine house, and prove me now herewith, saith the LORD of hosts, if I will not open you the windows of heaven, and pour you out a blessing, that there shall not be room enough to receive it.

Land Where My Father Died

Proverbs 4:7

Wisdom is the principal thing; therefore get wisdom: and with all thy getting, get understanding.

I recently talked with a friend who had just left her Sunday church service. I still think about her response to my question about the service. However, since I have heard her answer from others, I know her answer is typical of at least some services of today. My question was a simple one. I simply asked; "How was your service today"? Her answer was, "Great! We're a 100% tithing church now"

I was expecting to hear a mentioning of people being saved, delivered, healed, and raised from the dead or even a mentioning of what the preacher had preached. Have we forgotten? The building, tithes, offerings, songs, books and tapes are just instruments; tools to be used by the ministry. The real reason for church services should be to spread the Gospel of Jesus Christ. We cannot afford to lose focus because of money. Big buildings mean big mortgages. Big mortgages make us preach more about money. You cannot serve God and money. Besides, if you take money from the storehouse to pay the church mortgage or the pastor's car payment are you still robbing God?

How much prosperity is enough?

What does God say about wealth and riches? Can we reach a point where our quest for prosperity tips the scale? God gives and promises wealth and prosperity to believers. However, He is specific in his instructions to us. We should first seek God. We should also trust God enough to expect Him to provide for our needs and Godly desires by following His commandments. He instructs us to lend without expecting interest from our brethren, resist exploitation of others and avoid coveting things that belong to others. He instructs us to give when we are able and demonstrate genuine love and integrity before our fellow human beings.

Deuteronomy 8:18

But thou shalt remember the LORD thy God: for it is he that giveth thee power to get wealth, that he may establish his covenant which he sware unto thy fathers, as it is this day.

Matthew 6:33

But seek ye first the kingdom of God, and his righteousness; and all these things shall be added unto you.

Exodus 22:25

If thou lend money to any of my people that is poor by thee, thou shalt not be to him as an usurer, neither shalt thou lay upon him usury.

Luke 6:35

But love ye your enemies, and do good, and lend, hoping for nothing again; and your reward shall be great, and ye shall be the children of the Highest: for he is kind unto the unthankful and to the evil.

Land Where My Father Died

Luke 12:15

And he said unto them, Take heed, and beware of covetousness: for a man's life consisteth not in the abundance of the things which he possesseth.

Success vs. Wealth

Do we call it success or wealth? I often marvel at the amount of things that I have consumed over my lifetime. Maybe it is because I am getting older but I even look at my shoes now and wonder how much work it took for someone other than me to make them. How many people were involved in the making of the leather, the shoestrings, the rubber for the heels, the making of the insoles and the shoelaces, etc...? This may seem trivial to some but my point is that people made them - even if they just ran a machine. Too often, we forget that many others who are unknown to us contributed to our success. We humans are all dependent on one another. God said, "It is not good for man to be alone". I can now see why. We cannot make it by ourselves. Whether we are wealthy or poor, we are all dependent on someone else.

Joshua 1:8

This book of the law shall not depart out of thy mouth; but thou shalt meditate therein day and night, that thou mayest observe to do according to all that is written therein: for then thou shalt make thy way prosperous, and then thou shalt have good success.

Land Where My Father Died

Proverbs 13:11

Wealth gotten by vanity shall be diminished: but he that gathereth by labour shall increase.

Ecclesiastes 6:2

A man to whom God hath given riches, wealth, and honour, so that he wanteth nothing for his soul of all that he desireth, yet God giveth him not power to eat thereof, but a stranger eateth it: this is vanity, and it is an evil disease.

Land of Thy Pilgrim's Pride

Wars and rumors of wars

War – what is good for? Absolutely money! In fact, war is a "gold mine" for the rich. Just like those who exploit church members, some with the same mindset are pushing the buttons that lead us to war. One cannot ignore the fact that many modern wars have brought huge profits to some. These rich exploiters know that a nation will pay any amount available to protect its own security.

When our moral values sink and begin to serve at the discretion of money, we set ourselves up for catastrophe. *(T. M .Bell – 2007)*

The real cause of wars?

James 4

1 From whence come wars and fightings among you? come they not hence, even of your lusts that war in your members?

2 Ye lust, and have not: ye kill, and desire to have, and cannot obtain: ye fight and war, yet ye have not, because ye ask not.

3 Ye ask, and receive not, because ye ask amiss, that ye may consume it upon your lusts.

Follow the money. It is right there in our faces. WW1, WW2, and now the possible beginning of WW3 are being forced by the love of money or

Land Of Thy Pilgrim's Pride

its complement *"Power"*. Many wealthy gains are the direct result of WAR.

Proverbs 14:12 and Proverbs 16:25
There is a way which seemeth right unto a man, but the end thereof are the ways of death.

Proverbs 21:2
Every way of a man is right in his own eyes: but the LORD pondereth the hearts.

1 Corinthians 3:19
For the wisdom of this world is foolishness with God. For it is written, He taketh the wise in their own craftiness.

Modern wars

While the entire list of all wars in the last century is huge, listed below are just a few of which may be familiar today.   Just follow the money.

1948 Arab-Israeli War (Established modern Israel money)

1950 Korean War (Made in China or made in Korea money)

1956 Suez War (Power shift from British to US and USSR money)

1956 Vietnam War (France's money shift to China)

1967 Six Day War (Power shift to Israel – Control of water in the mid-east)

1970 War of Attrition (Israel tightens Control of water and land)

1971 Indo-Pakistani War (Power shift to India money)

Land Of Thy Pilgrim's Pride

1973 Yom Kippur War (More money shift to Israel)

1979 Soviet war in Afghanistan (Money Shift from USSR to US)

1980 Iran-Iraq War (Global Oil Money shift)

1982 Lebanon War (Money shift to Israel)

1982 Falklands War (Money reshuffled - Argentina to UK)

1987 Palestinian Intifada (Land shift to Israel)

1990 Gulf War (Oil Money)

1991 Yugoslav Wars (The conflict had its roots in various underlying political, economic and cultural problems as well as long-standing ethnic and religious tensions.)

1994 First Chechen War (Reshuffled Russia's Money)

1998 Kosovo War (The conflict had its roots in various underlying political, economic and cultural problems as well as long-standing ethnic and religious tensions.)

1999 Second Chechen War (Restoration of Russia's influence in the federal government)

2000 Al-Aqsa Intifada (The Israeli commerce has experienced much hardship, in particular because of the sharp drop in tourism.)

2001 U.S. invasion of Afghanistan (Halliburton)

2001 War on Terrorism (Halliburton)

2003 Iraq War (Halliburton)

We know in our heart of hearts that the Iraq war was about *"Oil"*. Yet many remain silent or appear complicit about what we know in our hearts is truly wrong. Just look at the profits Halliburton, ExxonMobil, BP, Shell and the other oil related companies are enjoying today. How

Land Of Thy Pilgrim's Pride

can nothing be said when so many lives are lost? Are our young soldiers being used as pawns by the rich?

I was so excited the day I joined the United States Air force in 1964. Some even called me "gung-ho". I was tops in my group in Basic Training and among the top of my tech school class. When I received my first promotion, I was ready to conquer the enemy. When I arrived in Thailand during the Viet Nam war, I was ready to do my duty. However, after watching the B-52's leave my base and drop bombs day after day, I wondered, why are we still fighting? I could drop 500 pounds of beer cans on a country the size of California every day for five years and expect to see the whole country covered with beer. We were dropping tons of big bombs daily but accomplishing very little. We were also using a great deal of oil. Could that have been the main purpose the of war? That sounds cynical but looking at the greedy exploits of *Big Oil* in Iraq, I now wonder. It makes one think. Is it merely coincidental that two Texan presidents have led us into two costly wars that made very little sense? After all, Texas **is** Big Oil.

Has Pilgrim's pride been replaced by Texas pride?

From Every Mountain Side

Poverty in America?

Poverty is relative. However, each occurrence of it declares a broken link in the supply and production chain. During one of my trips to the African bush country, I witnessed locals living blissfully in conditions that were unbearable to my compatriots. Nevertheless, their supply and production chains were intact. Even when their crops were affected by drastic weather conditions they endured by a common desire to spread their goods equitably. To them, poverty meant that someone failed to work or took more than their share. I saw a powerful spirit of peace and joy in the hearts and minds of the bush people.

According to the United States Census Bureau (2005), many Americans still live in poverty. In a rich country like America, what is a fair share of the wealth or what is an equitable share of the work? Since less than one percent of the people share more than 20% of America's wealth and 12.6% live in poverty, one would think that the supply and production chain in America is broken.

Just look at the following stats.

Highlights[16]

- The official poverty rate in 2005 was 12.6 percent.
- In 2005, 37.0 million people were in poverty.

---

[16] The mentioned data are taken from the Current Population Survey (CPS), 2006 Annual Social and Economic Supplement (ASEC), the source of official poverty estimates. The CPS ASEC is a sample survey of approximately 100,000 household nationwide. These data reflect conditions in calendar year 2005.

From Every Mountain Side

- Poverty for Blacks (24.9 percent) and Hispanics is 21.8 percent. The poverty rate decreased for non-Hispanic Whites to 8.3 percent in 2005
- The poverty rate in 2005 for children under 18 is 17.6 percent.
- In 2005, the number in poverty for people under 18 and people 18 to 64 years old was 12.9 million and 20.5 million, respectively.
- The number of seniors 65 and older in poverty was 3.6 million in 2005.

This Cannot Be True!

Based on these and other reports, 12.6 million American households, 11.2 percent of all American homes were afraid they might not be able to put enough food on the table. Please see The Changing Face of Poverty[17] (*By Octavio Blanco, CNN/Money staff writer*).

Millions of Americans live in poverty, while even more families are suffering, and hunger is increasing. At risk is access to food, shelter and healthcare for many Americans. Homelessness continues to rise in major American cities. Meanwhile, many others are illegally crossing American borders to pursue a better life. Some say as many as 12 to 20 million people may be living in America illegally. The net effect is that the poverty level is growing substantially beyond the Census Bureau's ability to measure and report.

---

[17] December 30, 2004: 1:14 PM EST. *By Octavio Blanco, CNN/Money staff writer*

From Every Mountain Side

We normally equate poverty and hunger with problems that exist in the *Third World*. However, while over 400 Americans are living comfortably with a net worth of more than a $1 Billion, millions of others are trying to make it on annual incomes of less than $9,000. Just imagine – these 400 billionaires are able to spend $100,000 for every dollar spent by the 30 millions other people who are living in poverty. I suggest that America looks different to these two classes of people. No! Freedom is not ringing from every mountainside.

Meanwhile, the rich gets richer...

Currently, many companies are involved in massive worker lay-offs in America while sending jobs to other countries. Once flourishing cities like Detroit, Cleveland and Saint Louis are being ruined. This would not be so bad if shortages were fair-minded. However, while workers are loosing jobs and taking pay cuts, many already rich corporate bosses are receiving huge salaries, bonuses, stock options and other compensations packages. Additionally, in their quest to please already rich shareholders, these bosses are also pressuring labor unions. Unions are also declining both in membership and influence on American policies. One would conclude that job growth in countries like China, India, and Mexico are linked to the decline in America jobs. In the end, their gains are our losses.

I can remember when my father and his friends hoped for a good union job with good wages, good medical and good retirement benefits. These days, many American workers are just happy to find any work available. Regretfully, many jobs remaining in America are also decaying in terms of quality, quantity, benefits and job security. Many good jobs are gone forever.

Enough is Enough

In 2001, as a director of consulting and engineering services, I watched my company lose contract after contract to information technology companies from India. In many cases, our products were clearly superior but were rejected solely because American labor rates were higher. The lost job opportunities had a demoralizing impact on the newly hired American Engineering graduates. They had believed that after four years of hard study, work would be available. What a pity. They could not have known that their dreams would be cut off by the rich and greedy. I later learned many of the credentials used by the workers in India were fake.

In March 2006, the Organization for Economic Co-operation and Development published a report showing that China's exports of information and communications technology, including laptops, mobile phones and digital cameras, grew in 2004 by more than 46 percent to $180 billion, surpassing U.S. exports of $149 billion. China's annual Gross Domestic Product (GDP) has grown from $547 Billion in 1980 to

From Every Mountain Side

around $10 Trillion in 2005. Meanwhile, U. S. real GDP rose from $9 Trillion to $13 Trillion during the same period.[22] Many of our lost jobs are being done by the Chinese now. The following list is from CIA World Factbook (April 2006) and ranks the 20 top countries in terms of annual GDP. It is clear the some countries have improved their ranking due to an arrival of American jobs.

Rank	Country	GDP (PPP) $m
—	World	65,000,000
1	United States	12,980,000
—	European Union	12,820,000
2	People's Republic of China	10,000,000
3	Japan	4,220,000
4	India	4,042,000
5	Germany	2,585,000
6	United Kingdom	1,903,000
7	France	1,871,000
8	Italy	1,727,000
9	Russia	1,723,000
10	Brazil	1,616,000
11	South Korea	1,180,000
12	Canada	1,165,000
13	Mexico	1,134,000
14	Spain	1,070,000
15	Indonesia	935,000
16	Republic of China(Taiwan)	668,300
17	Australia	666,300
18	Turkey	627,200

[22] CIA World Factbook

From Every Mountain Side

Rank	Country	GDP (PPP) $m
19	Iran	610,400
20	Argentina	599,100

(World Ranking - CIA World Factbook 2006)

Means Justifying The End

Is the increased poverty rate it worth it? Should the rich continue to get richer? According to Forbes magazine's 2006 and the CIA report shown above, the net worth of 793 billionaires is more than Gross Domestic Products (GDP) Purchasing Power Parity (ppp) of every single one of 230 countries except for the U. S., Japan, China, and India. Moreover, their net worth of $2.6 trillion is bigger than the combined GDP of 167 of the world poorest countries.

Let Freedom Ring

Cups Overflowing

On Becoming Little Gods

Genesis 3:22

And the LORD God said, Behold, the man is become as one of us, to know good and evil: and now, lest he put forth his hand, and take also of the tree of life, and eat, and live for ever:

Who are the rich?

Let us think about some of the richest people in America. They are not gods but many treat them as such. Yes, they have a pile of money but they are not to be feared or reverenced. You cannot serve both God and Money.

When Famine Comes!

Genesis 47:15

And when money failed in the land of Egypt, and in the land of Canaan, all the Egyptians came unto Joseph, and said, Give us bread: for why should we die in thy presence? for the money faileth.

Let Freedom Ring

Considering this concentration of wealth among a few, what can we expect from them if famine should hit this country? What happens when our money fails? What are the plans for redistribution if needed? Should these questions be asked? Some of the most wealthiest are thinking ahead. They know the strategic meaning of *charity*.

Luke 12:13-59

The Parable of the Rich Fool

13 And one of the company said unto him, Master, speak to my brother, that he divide the inheritance with me.

14 And he said unto him, Man, who made me a judge or a divider over you?

15 And he said unto them, Take heed, and beware of covetousness: for a man's life consisteth not in the abundance of the things which he possesseth.

16 And he spake a parable unto them, saying, The ground of a certain rich man brought forth plentifully:

17 And he thought within himself, saying, What shall I do, because I have no room where to bestow my fruits?

18 And he said, This will I do: I will pull down my barns, and build greater; and there will I bestow all my fruits and my goods.

19 And I will say to my soul, Soul, thou hast much goods laid up for many years; take thine ease, eat, drink, and be merry.

20 But God said unto him, Thou fool, this night thy soul shall be required of thee: then whose shall those things be, which thou hast provided?

21   So is he that layeth up treasure for himself, and is not rich toward God.

Do Not Worry

22   And he said unto his disciples, Therefore I say unto you, Take no thought for your life, what ye shall eat; neither for the body, what ye shall put on.

23   The life is more than meat, and the body is more than raiment.

24   Consider the ravens: for they neither sow nor reap; which neither have storehouse nor barn; and God feedeth them: how much more are ye better than the fowls?

25   And which of you with taking thought can add to his stature one cubit?

26   If ye then be not able to do that thing which is least, why take ye thought for the rest?

27   Consider the lilies how they grow: they toil not, they spin not; and yet I say unto you, that Solomon in all his glory was not arrayed like one of these.

28   If then God so clothe the grass, which is to day in the field, and to morrow is cast into the oven; how much more will he clothe you, O ye of little faith?

29   And seek not ye what ye shall eat, or what ye shall drink, neither be ye of doubtful mind.

30   For all these things do the nations of the world seek after: and your Father knoweth that ye have need of these things.

31   But rather seek ye the kingdom of God; and all these things shall be added unto you.

32 Fear not, little flock; for it is your Father's good pleasure to give you the kingdom.

33 Sell that ye have, and give alms; provide yourselves bags which wax not old, a treasure in the heavens that faileth not, where no thief approacheth, neither moth corrupteth.

34 For where your treasure is, there will your heart be also.

Watchfulness

35 Let your loins be girded about, and your lights burning;

36 And ye yourselves like unto men that wait for their lord, when he will return from the wedding; that when he cometh and knocketh, they may open unto him immediately.

37 Blessed are those servants, whom the lord when he cometh shall find watching: verily I say unto you, that he shall gird himself, and make them to sit down to meat, and will come forth and serve them.

38 And if he shall come in the second watch, or come in the third watch, and find them so, blessed are those servants.

39 And this know, that if the goodman of the house had known what hour the thief would come, he would have watched, and not have suffered his house to be broken through.

40 Be ye therefore ready also: for the Son of man cometh at an hour when ye think not.

41 Then Peter said unto him, Lord, speakest thou this parable unto us, or even to all?

Let Freedom Ring

42 And the Lord said, Who then is that faithful and wise steward, whom his lord shall make ruler over his household, to give them their portion of meat in due season?

43 Blessed is that servant, whom his lord when he cometh shall find so doing.

44 Of a truth I say unto you, that he will make him ruler over all that he hath.

45 But and if that servant say in his heart, My lord delayeth his coming; and shall begin to beat the menservants and maidens, and to eat and drink, and to be drunken;

46 The lord of that servant will come in a day when he looketh not for him, and at an hour when he is not aware, and will cut him in sunder, and will appoint him his portion with the unbelievers.

47 And that servant, which knew his lord's will, and prepared not himself, neither did according to his will, shall be beaten with many stripes.

48 But he that knew not, and did commit things worthy of stripes, shall be beaten with few stripes. For unto whomsoever much is given, of him shall be much required: and to whom men have committed much, of him they will ask the more.

Not Peace but Division

49 I am come to send fire on the earth; and what will I, if it be already kindled?

50 But I have a baptism to be baptized with; and how am I straitened till it be accomplished!

51   Suppose ye that I am come to give peace on earth? I tell you, Nay; but rather division:

52   For from henceforth there shall be five in one house divided, three against two, and two against three.

53   The father shall be divided against the son, and the son against the father; the mother against the daughter, and the daughter against the mother; the mother in law against her daughter in law, and the daughter in law against her mother in law.

Interpreting the Times

54   And he said also to the people, When ye see a cloud rise out of the west, straightway ye say, There cometh a shower; and so it is.

55   And when ye see the south wind blow, ye say, There will be heat; and it cometh to pass.

56   Ye hypocrites, ye can discern the face of the sky and of the earth; but how is it that ye do not discern this time?

57   Yea, and why even of yourselves judge ye not what is right?

58   When thou goest with thine adversary to the magistrate, as thou art in the way, give diligence that thou mayest be delivered from him; lest he hale thee to the judge, and the judge deliver thee to the officer, and the officer cast thee into prison.

59   I tell thee, thou shalt not depart thence, till thou hast paid the very last mite.

Let Freedom Ring

Strategic Charities – Thanks to the Givers

History's Top 10 U.S. Philanthropists[23]

Some inherited wealth, others worked hard, many never finished High School or college, but they are rich and they give. Some give because of religious beliefs and feelings of civic responsibility. Some appear to believe in philanthropy, while others seem to give away money impulsively. Nevertheless, according to published reports, everyone on the list shares two traits: They were extremely rich and they have given a lot of their money to charity—at least $2.8 billion each in today's dollars.

America's 10 Greatest Givers

1. Warren Buffet (1930 -)

As a young man, Warren Buffet became interested in business and investing while working at his father's stock brokerage firm and has amassed one of the biggest fortunes in the United States. In 2006, he announced the largest gift in U.S. history when he agreed that he would give more than $30 billion to the Gates Foundation. According to reports, he plans to transfer some of his investment firm stocks, Berkshire Hathaway, to the Gates foundation. His habit of seeking the best-run companies for investing his money led him to the well-run Gates

---

[23] From Wikipedia, the free encyclopedia

Let Freedom Ring

Foundation. Buffet and his late wife, Susie, have given billions to their own foundation, which supports charities dealing with reproductive rights and nuclear weapons reduction.

2. Bill Gates (1955 -)

Bill Gates, the son of a Seattle attorney and his schoolteacher wife, dropped out of Harvard and co-founded a software company called Microsoft. He and his wife Melinda have contributed more than $26 billion to their foundation, which was already the largest in the world before a pledge from Warren Buffet increased its worth to $60 billion. Because of its size, the foundation faces a huge challenge in giving away its money wisely. Consequently, Gates announced that he would step down from his daily duties at Microsoft in July 2008 to devote himself full-time to his philanthropy. Among the foundation's initiatives is a $1.5 billion program to vaccinate people against diphtheria and other common diseases.

Let Freedom Ring

According to public records, the Gates foundation operates on the following 15 philanthropic principles:

1. The interests and passions of the Gates family drive the foundation.

2. Philanthropy plays an important but limited role.

3. The foundation believes that science and technology have great potential to improve lives around the world.

4. The foundation funds and shapes — others act and implement.

5. The foundation focuses on limited, prioritized, and most neglected issues.

6. The foundation will identify a specific point of intervention and apply its efforts against a theory of change.

7. The foundation takes risks, makes big bets, and moves with urgency. They are in it for the long haul.

8. The foundation advocates vigorously but responsibly in focused areas.

9. The foundation acts humbly and mindfully in actions and words. It pledges to seek and heed the counsel of outside voices.

Let Freedom Ring

10. Grantees are treated as valued partners, and ultimate beneficiaries are treated with respect.

11. Information and results are shared.

12. The foundation demands ethical behavior.

13. The foundation's board treats each other as valued colleagues.

14. The foundation mission is to increase opportunity and equity for those most in need.

15. The foundation leaves room for growth and change.

3. John D. Rockefeller (1839 – 1937)

Rockefeller was born in Richford, N.Y. In his first job as a bookkeeper, he developed the habit of tithing 10 percent of his income to his church. His percentage increased, as he grew wealthier. He bought out other oil companies to develop Standard Oil, which for a time controlled the mining, piping and refining of U.S. petroleum. Rockefeller primarily gave to public health and education. Among other things, his gifts helped eradicate hookworm disease, which had long plagued the South. He was remembered for many years for his habit of giving a dime to every child he met.

Let Freedom Ring

4. Andrew Carnegie (1835 – 1919)

Carnegie was born in Scotland in 1835 and became the family breadwinner at age 12 after they had moved to the United States. Carnegie was working his way up the ladder at Pennsylvania Railroad when he saw opportunities in the iron and steel industries. He believed that he had a civic responsibility to share his wealth, and his writings stimulated other new millionaires of the time to follow his example. He favored helping people help themselves; rather than giving to the poor, he built libraries (more than 2,500 worldwide) as well as parks, concert halls, and museums. In addition, he created the Carnegie Endowment for International Peace and the Carnegie Corporation of New York, a charitable foundation.

5. Gordon E. Moore (1929 -)

The creator of the Intel microprocessor chip grew up in San Francisco. An engineer, chemist, and entrepreneur, he founded Intel in 1968 with a venture capital grant, building the company into one of the early Silicon Valley success stories. He and his wife Betty donated half his Intel holdings to start the Gordon E. and Betty I. Moore Foundation to support the environment, scientific research, and higher education as well as local San Francisco causes. It has made substantial grants to the California Institute of Technology and the University of California at Berkeley, among other institutions. Moore has

Let Freedom Ring

expressed concern about over-development and the continuing loss of natural environment in many parts of the world.

6. Robert Woods Johnson II (1893 - 1938)

The son of the founder of Johnson & Johnson health care products company grew up in New Brunswick, N.J. Although his father died when he was 16 years old, Johnson worked his way up the ranks in the company and assumed the presidency in 1932. Under his direction, the company grew from $11 million to $700 million in annual sales. He created one of the world's largest foundations dedicated to helping the needy in 1936. Today, the foundation seeks to improve the quality of medical care as well as Americans' access to it.

7. John D. Rockefeller Jr. (1874 – 1960)

Rockefeller's son carried on his father's support of public health and education, but also gave to emergency relief efforts during the Depression. The younger Rockefeller is also remembered for his environmental and preservation work. He helped restore colonial Williamsburg, Virginia. and bought or helped to buy some of the crown jewels of the national park system, including Acadia National Park in Maine and Virgin Islands National Park in St. John, and Grand Teton National Park in Wyoming.

8. George Soros (1930 -)

The billionaire financier was born in 1930 to a Jewish family in Budapest, Hungary and lived for a time under Nazi and later

Communist rule. He studied at the London School of Economics and worked for a British investment firm before starting the Quantum hedge fund in New York. In 1979, he began giving to help black students attend college in South Africa, and later expanded his philanthropy through his Open Society Institute to promote a free press and other democratic institutions in repressive societies around the world. After the collapse of the Soviet Union, Soros gave more than $2 billion to promote market economies in the former Soviet Republics.

9. Henry Ford (1863 – 1947)

Ford grew up on a farm near Dearborn, Michigan, but his interests were more mechanical than agricultural. After several engineering jobs, he started Ford Motor Company, which transformed the auto industry with efficient assembly-line production. Ford distrusted many forms of traditional philanthropy. He believed that charitable acts only humble the recipient and cause him to resent the giver. As he put it - "Give a man something and you make an enemy of him for life". During his lifetime, he was known for his philanthropy in Michigan, building a hospital, and creating a museum and historical village. He started the Ford Foundation in 1936 with his son, Edsel. Today, it is one of the largest American foundations.

10.   John D. McArthur (1897 – 1978)

MacArthur, who grew up in a Pennsylvania coal-mining town, built his fortune selling inexpensive life insurance.   He expanded Bankers Life and Casualty Co. into a multibillion-dollar business, and moved into real estate, broadcasting, and other fields.   He and his wife Catherine in 1978 created the foundation that bears their name, which emphasizes health, education, and environmental concerns.   A signature of the foundation is its MacArthur Fellows program, which awards unsolicited $500,000 grants, often called "genius grants", to people that it considers will be able to use the money to make a difference in science, art, philanthropy or other endeavors.

The Ambiance of Riches

Have you ever wondered how much money billionaires spend? Their power in their local communities is undeniable. California leads the way with 90 billionaires and most are living near Los Angeles. New York is next with 55 billionares living mainly around New York city. Texas lists 36 billionares and many live around the Dallas and Fort Worth areas. While Michael Dell tops the list, "big oil" money can be seen throughout Texas.

With the growth in technology companies like Microsoft, McCaw Cellular and Amazon and classie coffee companies like Starbucks, came nine billionaires who are now living in the Seattle, Washington area. The ambiance of billionaires has produced more than 118,000 millionaires in Seattle and surrounding areas. When I first moved to Seattle in 1974, one could purchase a house on Mercer Island for less than $200,000. Now many homes are selling for more than $20 million. The effect on the underprivileged is devastating. The poor cannot afford to purchase homes. Thus, a subtle class system is growing.

Following is a list ranking 400 richest Americans. Ranking is based on an article from Forbes Magazine's 2006 Edition.

California's Billionaires

Rank	Name	Net Worth ($Bil)	Age	Residence	Source
4	Lawrence Joseph Ellison	19.5	62	Redwood City, CA	Oracle
12	Sergey Brin	14.1	33	Palo Alto, CA	Google
13	Larry E Page	14	33	San Francisco, CA	Google

400 Riches Americans – *Source , From Forbes Magazine 2006*

Rank	Name	Net Worth ($Bil)	Age	Residence	Source
26	Kirk Kerkorian	9	89	Los Angeles, CA	Investments, Casinos
27	Donald L Bren	8.5	74	Newport Beach, CA	Real Estate
35	Sumner M Redstone	7.5	83	Beverly Hills, CA	Viacom
42	Eli Broad	5.8	73	Los Angeles, CA	Investments
45	Eric Schmidt	5.2	51	Atherton, CA	Google
49	Steven Paul Jobs	4.9	51	Palo Alto, CA	Apple Computer, Pixar
50	Charles R Schwab	4.6	69	Atherton, CA	Discount Stock Brokerage
50	David Geffen	4.6	63	Malibu, CA	Movies, M
52	Charles Bartlett Johnson	4.5	73	San Mateo, CA	Franklin Resources
59	David Howard Murdock	4.2	83	Los Angeles, CA	Investments
61	Bradley Wayne Hughes	4.1	73	Malibu, CA	Public Storage
68	Rupert Harris Johnson Jr	3.7	65	San Mateo, CA	Franklin Resources
70	George Lucas	3.6	62	Marin County, CA	Star Wars
77	Patrick Soon-Shiong	3.4	54	Los Angeles, CA	Generic Drugs
77	Gordon Earle Moore	3.4	77	Woodside, CA	Intel
83	Steven Udvar-Hazy	3.1	60	Beverly Hills, CA	International Lease Finance
85	A Jerrold Perenchio	3	75	Bel Air, CA	Univision
85	Roland Arnall	3	67	Holmby Hills, CA	Mortgage Banking
94	Steven Allen Spielberg	2.9	59	Pacific Palisades, CA	Movies
98	Haim Saban	2.8	61	Beverly Hills, CA	Television
103	Riley P Bechtel	2.7	54	San Francisco, CA	Engineering, Construction
103	Stephen Davison Bechtel Jr	2.7	81	San Francisco, CA	Engineering, Construction
107	George R Roberts	2.6	62	San Francisco,	Leveraged Buyouts

400 Riches Americans – *Source , From Forbes Magazine 2006*

Rank	Name	Net Worth ($Bil)	Age	Residence	Source
				CA	
117	Ronald Burkle	2.5	53	Los Angeles, CA	Supermarkets, Investments
117	David Filo	2.5	40	Palo Alto, CA	Yahoo
131	John Albert Sobrato	2.4	67	Atherton, CA	Real Estate
133	Gordon Peter Getty	2.3	73	San Francisco, CA	Inheritance, Oil
140	Jess Stonestreet Jackson	2.2	76	Healdsburg, CA	Jackson Fay Wines
140	Jerry Yang	2.2	37	Los Altos, CA	Yahoo
140	Alfred Mann	2.2	80	Los Angeles, CA	Inventor, Entrepreneur
140	Ernest S Rady	2.2	69	San Diego, CA	Banking, Insurance
153	Michael Robert Milken	2.1	60	Los Angeles, CA	Investments
153	William Randolph Hearst III	2.1	57	San Francisco, CA	Hearst Corp
160	Tom T Gores	2	42	Beverly Hills, CA	Leveraged Buyouts
160	Henry Thompson Nicholas III	2	47	Laguna Hills, CA	Broadcom
160	David Whitmire Hearst Jr	2	61	Los Angeles, CA	Hearst Corp
160	George Randolph Hearst Jr	2	79	Los Angeles, CA	Hearst Corp
160	Anthony Pritzker	2	45	Los Angeles, CA	Hotels, Investments
160	Daniel Pritzker	2	47	Marin County, CA	Hotels, Investments
160	Henry Samueli	2	52	Newport Beach, CA	Broadcom
160	Charles H Brandes	2	63	San Diego, CA	Money Management
160	Phoebe Hearst Cooke	2	79	San Francisco, CA	Hearst Corp
160	John A Pritzker	2	53	San Francisco, CA	Hotels, Investments
189	Omid Kordestani	1.9	42	Atherton, CA	Google

400 Riches Americans – *Source , From Forbes Magazine 2006*

Rank	Name	Net Worth ($Bil)	Age	Residence	Source
189	John Edward Anderson	1.9	89	Bel Air, CA	Investments
189	Franklin Otis Booth Jr	1.9	83	Los Angeles, CA	Berkshire Hathaway
197	Edward P Roski Jr	1.8	67	Los Angeles, CA	Real Estate
204	Irwin Mark Jacobs	1.7	72	La Jolla, CA	Qualcomm
204	Theodore W Waitt	1.7	43	San Diego, CA	Gateway
204	Ray Milton Dolby	1.7	73	San Francisco, CA	Dolby Laboratories
215	Archie Aldis "Red" Emmerson	1.6	77	Anderson, CA	Timberland, Lumber Ls
215	Louis L Gonda	1.6	58	Beverly Hills, CA	International Lease Finance
215	Charles T Munger	1.6	82	Los Angeles, CA	Berkshire Hathaway
215	George Leon Argyros	1.6	69	Newport Beach, CA	Real Estate, Investments
215	Igor Olenicoff	1.6	64	Newport Beach, CA	Real Estate
242	Alan I Casden	1.5	60	Beverly Hills, CA	Real Estate
242	Manny Mashouf & Family	1.5	68	Brisbane, CA	Bebe
242	Kavitark Ram Shriram	1.5	50	Mountain View, CA	Google
242	John P Morgridge	1.5	73	Portola Valley, CA	Cisco
242	Thomas M Siebel	1.5	53	San Mateo, CA	Siebel Systems
278	Gary Karlin Michelson	1.4	57	Los Angeles, CA	Medical Patents
297	Leslie L Gonda	1.3	86	Beverly Hills, CA	International Lease Finance
297	Robert Addison Day	1.3	62	Los Angeles, CA	Money Management
297	Ernest Gallo & Family	1.3	97	Modesto, CA	Wine
297	John J Fisher	1.3	45	San Francisco, CA	Gap
297	Scott D Cook	1.3	54	Woodside, CA	Intuit
297	Kenneth L Fisher	1.3	55	Woodside, CA	Money Management

400 Riches Americans – *Source , From Forbes Magazine 2006*

Rank	Name	Net Worth ($Bil)	Age	Residence	Source
322	Carl Edwin Berg	1.2	69	Atherton, CA	Real Estate
322	Margaret C Whitman	1.2	50	Atherton, CA	Ebay
322	Alec Gores	1.2	53	Beverly Hills, CA	Leveraged Buyouts
322	William H Gross	1.2	62	Laguna Beach, CA	Bonds
322	Roy Edward Disney	1.2	76	Los Angeles, CA	Walt Disney
322	Timothy Blixseth	1.2	56	Rancho Mirage, CA	Timberland, Real Estate
322	Robert J Fisher	1.2	53	San Francisco, CA	Gap
322	William Sydney Fisher	1.2	49	San Francisco, CA	Gap
322	Robert Allen Naify	1.2	84	San Francisco, CA	Movie Theaters
354	Jonathan Lovelace Jr & Family	1.1	79	Los Angeles, CA	Mutual Funds
354	Joyce Raley Teel	1.1	75	Sacramento, CA	Supermarkets
354	Elizabeth S Wiskemann	1.1	NA	San Rafael, CA	Mutual Funds
354	Alexander Gus Spanos & Family	1.1	83	Stockton, CA	Real Estate
374	Weili Dai	1	45	Los Altos Hills, CA	Semiconductors
374	Sehat Sutardja	1	45	Los Altos Hills, CA	Semico
374	William Barron Hilton	1	78	Los Angeles, CA	Hotels, Casinos
374	George Joseph	1	85	Los Angeles, CA	Insurance
374	Kenneth G Langone	1	71	Sands Point, NY	Investments
374	Thomas J Barrack	1	59	Santa Barbara, CA	Colony Capital
374	L John Doerr	1	55	Woodside, CA	Venture Capital

400 Riches Americans – *Source , From Forbes Magazine 2006*

New York's Billionaires

Rank	Name	Net Worth ($Bil)	Age	Residence	Source
19	David Hamilton Koch	12	66	New York, NY	Oil, Commodities
24	Carl Icahn	9.7	70	New York, NY	Leveraged Buyouts
27	George Soros	8.5	76	Westchester, NY	Hedge Funds
32	Keith Rupert Murdoch	7.7	75	New York, NY	News Corp
38	Samuel Irving Newhouse Jr	7.3	78	New York, NY	Publishing
40	Ronald Owen Perelman	7	63	New York, NY	Leveraged Buyouts
40	Leonard Blavatnik	7	49	New York, NY	Access Industries
44	Michael Rubens Bloomberg	5.3	64	New York, NY	Bloomberg L.P.
64	James H Simons	4	68	East Setauket, NY	Hedge Funds
66	Ralph Lauren	3.9	66	New York, NY	Fashion
68	Leonard Norman Stern	3.7	68	New York, NY	Real Estate
73	Paul Milstein & Family	3.5	84	New York, NY	Emigrant, Real Estate
73	Stephen A Schwarzman	3.5	59	New York, NY	Investments
77	Joan H Tisch	3.4	80	New York, NY	Loews
80	Edgar M Bronfman Sr	3.2	77	New York, NY	Liquor

400 Riches Americans – *Source , From Forbes Magazine 2006*

Rank	Name	Net Worth ($Bil)	Age	Residence	Source
85	Bruce Kovner	3	61	New York, NY	Hedge Funds
94	Leonard Alan Lauder	2.9	73	New York, NY	Estee Lauder
94	Donald John Trump	2.9	60	New York, NY	Real Estate
103	Ronald Steven Lauder	2.7	62	New York, NY	Estee Lauder
107	Henry R Kravis	2.6	62	New York, NY	Leveraged Buyouts
107	David Rockefeller Sr	2.6	91	New York, NY	Standard Oil, Banking
117	Leona Mindy Rosenthal Helmsley	2.5	86	New York, NY	Real Estate
117	Stephen M Ross	2.5	66	New York, NY	Real Estate
117	Mortimer Benjamin Zuckerman	2.5	69	New York, NY	Real Estate, Media
117	David Gottesman	2.5	80	Rye, NY	Investments
133	Charles Francis Dolan & Family	2.3	79	Oyster Bay, NY	Cablevision Systems
160	Herbert Anthony Allen Jr	2	66	New York, NY	Investment Banking
160	Leon Black	2	55	New York, NY	Leveraged Buyouts
160	Stanley Druckenmiller	2	54	New York, NY	Hedge Funds
160	Austin Hearst	2	54	New York, NY	Hearst Corp
160	Tamir Sapir	2	59	New York, NY	Real Estate

400 Riches Americans – Source , From Forbes Magazine 2006

Rank	Name	Net Worth ($Bil)	Age	Residence	Source
189	Wilma Stein Tisch & Family	1.9	79	New York, NY	Loews
204	Sheldon Henry Solow	1.7	78	New York, NY	Real Estate
204	Blase Thomas Golisano	1.7	64	Victor, NY	Paychex
242	Stewart Rahr	1.5	60	New York, NY	Kinray
242	Sanford Weill	1.5	73	New York, NY	Citigroup
242	Daniel Morton Ziff	1.5	34	New York, NY	Inheritance, Hedge Funds
242	Dirk Edward Ziff	1.5	42	New York, NY	Inheritance, Hedge Funds
242	Robert David Ziff	1.5	40	New York, NY	Inheritance, Hedge Funds
278	Alan Gerry	1.4	77	Liberty, NY	Cable Television
278	Thomas Haskell Lee	1.4	62	New York, NY	Leveraged Buyouts
278	Steven Roth	1.4	64	New York, NY	Real Estate
297	Nelson Peltz	1.3	64	Bedford, NY	Leveraged Buyouts
297	Barry Diller	1.3	64	New York, NY	InterActiveCorp
297	Herbert Siegel	1.3	78	New York, NY	Television
322	Jerome Spiegel Kohlberg Jr	1.2	81	Mt Kisco, NY	Leveraged Buyouts
322	Israel Englander	1.2	58	New York, NY	Hedge Funds

400 Riches Americans – *Source , From Forbes Magazine 2006*

Rank	Name	Net Worth ($Bil)	Age	Residence	Source
322	J Christopher Flowers	1.2	48	New York, NY	Investments
322	Michael Jaharis	1.2	78	New York, NY	Pharmaceuticals
354	James Cayne	1.1	72	New York, NY	Bear Stearns
374	Jeremy Maurice Jacobs Sr	1	66	East Aurora, NY	Sports Concessions
374	Leonard Litwin	1	91	Great Neck, NY	Real Estate
374	Ira L Rennert	1	72	New York, NY	Investments
374	Julian H Robertson Jr	1	74	New York, NY	Money Management, Wine
374	David E Shaw	1	55	New York, NY	Hedge Funds

Texas' Billionares

Rank	Name	Net Worth ($Bil)	Age	Residence	Source
9	Michael Dell	15.5	41	Austin, TX	Dell
9	Alice L Walton	15.5	57	Fort Worth, TX	Wal-Mart
35	Dan L Duncan	7.5	73	Houston, TX	Energy
43	Robert Muse Bass	5.5	58	Fort Worth, TX	Oil, Investments
45	Robert Rowling	5.2	53	Dallas, TX	Oil & Gas, Investments
57	Henry Ross Perot	4.3	76	Dallas, TX	Computer Services, Real Estate
61	Harold Clark Simmons	4.1	75	Dallas, TX	Investments
73	Ray Lee Hunt	3.5	63	Dallas, TX	Oil, Real Estate
85	Lee Marshall Bass	3	50	Fort Worth, TX	Oil, Investments
85	Sid Richardson Bass	3	63	Fort Worth, TX	Oil, Investments
98	Richard Kinder	2.8	62	Houston, TX	Pipelines

400 Riches Americans – *Source , From Forbes Magazine 2006*

Rank	Name	Net Worth ($Bil)	Age	Residence	Source
103	T Boone Pickens	2.7	78	Dallas, TX	Oil & Gas, Investments
117	Edward Perry Bass	2.5	61	Fort Worth, TX	Oil, Investments
117	Richard Edward Rainwater	2.5	62	Fort Worth, TX	Real Estate, Energy, Insurance
117	George Phydias Mitchell	2.5	87	The Woodlands, TX	Mitchell Energy
133	Mark Cuban	2.3	48	Dallas, TX	Broadcast.Com
140	Charles C Butt & Family	2.2	68	San Antonio, TX	Supermarkets
215	Gerald J Ford	1.6	62	Dallas, TX	Banking
242	Trevor Rees-Jones	1.5	56	Dallas, TX	Oil
242	Robert C Mcnair	1.5	69	Houston, TX	Energy, Sports
242	Fayez Shalaby Sarofim	1.5	77	Houston, TX	Money Management
278	Todd R Wagner	1.4	46	Dallas, TX	Broadcast.Com
278	Joseph Dahr Jamail Jr	1.4	80	Houston, TX	Lawsuits
278	Tracy W Krohn	1.4	52	Houston, TX	W&T Offshore
278	Christopher Goldsbury	1.4	63	San Antonio, TX	Salsa
297	Jerral W Jones	1.3	63	Dallas, TX	Dallas Cowboys
297	Anne Windfohr Marion	1.3	67	Fort Worth, TX	Inheritance, Oil
297	Billy Joe "Red" Mccombs	1.3	78	San Antonio, TX	Radio, Oil, Real Estate
322	Kenny A Troutt	1.2	58	Dallas, TX	Excel Communications
322	Leslie Alexander	1.2	63	Houston, TX	First Marblehead
322	Thomas Friedkin	1.2	71	Houston, TX	Gulf States Toyota
322	Robert Drayton Mclane Jr	1.2	70	Temple, TX	Wal-Mart, Logistics
354	Timothy Headington	1.1	56	Dallas, TX	Oil, Investments
354	Samuel Wyly	1.1	71	Dallas, TX	Investments
374	William Alvin Moncrief Jr	1	86	Fort Worth, TX	Oil
374	Jeffrey Hildebrand	1	47	Houston, TX	Oil

400 Riches Americans – *Source , From Forbes Magazine 2006*

Florida's Billionaires

Rank	Name	Net Worth ($Bil)	Age	Residence	Source
25	John Werner Kluge	9.1	92	Palm Beach, FL	Metromedia
48	Micky Arison	5	57	Bal Harbour, FL	Carnival Cruises
98	Maurice Raymond Greenberg	2.8	81	Ocean Reef, FL	American International Group
131	James Martin Moran	2.4	88	Deerfield Beach, FL	Auto Distributorships
153	H Wayne Huizenga	2.1	68	Fort Lauderdale, FL	Investments
160	Malcolm Glazer & Family	2	78	Palm Beach, FL	Sports Teams, Real Estate
189	Robert E "Ted" Turner	1.9	67	Lamont, FL	Cable Television
189	S Daniel Abraham	1.9	82	Palm Beach, FL	Slim-Fast
197	Jorge M Perez	1.8	57	Miami, FL	Condos
204	Arthur L Williams Jr	1.7	64	Palm Beach, FL	Insurance
215	John Hugh Macmillan III	1.6	78	Hillsboro Beach, FL	Inheritance
215	Albert Lee Ueltschi	1.6	89	Vero Beach, FL	Flight safety International
242	James C France	1.5	62	Daytona Beach, FL	Auto Racing
242	William C France Jr	1.5	74	Daytona Beach, FL	Auto Racing
242	Fred Deluca	1.5	58	Fort Lauderdale, FL	Subway
242	Robert E Rich Jr	1.5	65	Islamorada, FL	Nondairy Creamer
242	George L Lindemann & Family	1.5	70	Palm Beach, FL	Investments
242	Edward John Debartolo Jr	1.5	59	Tampa, FL	Shopping Centers
278	Peter Benjamin Lewis	1.4	72	Coconut Grove, FL	Progressive Corp
278	Phillip Frost	1.4	69	Miami, FL	Ivax
297	Charlotte Colket Weber	1.3	63	Ocala, FL	Inheritance
297	William Ingraham Koch	1.3	66	Palm Beach, FL	Oil
322	Edmund Newton Ansin	1.2	70	Miami Beach, FL	Sunbeam Broadcasting

400 Riches Americans – *Source , From Forbes Magazine 2006*

Rank	Name	Net Worth ($Bil)	Age	Residence	Source
322	Wilbur L Ross Jr	1.2	68	Palm Beach, FL	Leveraged Buyouts
354	James H Clark	1.1	62	Palm Beach, FL	Netscape
374	Michael E Heisley Sr	1	69	Jupiter Island, FL	Manufacturing
374	William Morean	1	51	St Petersburg, FL	Ja Circuit

Illinois' Billionaires

Rank	Name	Net Worth ($Bil)	Age	Residence	Source
52	H Ty Warner	4.5	62	Chicago, IL	Beanie Babies
52	Samuel Zell	4.5	65	Chicago, IL	Real Estate, Private Equity
61	Lester Crown & Family	4.1	81	Wilmette, IL	Investments
85	Matthew Bucksbaum & Family	3	80	Chicago, IL	Real Estate
133	Thomas J Pritzker	2.3	56	Chicago, IL	Hotels, Investments
153	Penny Pritzker	2.1	47	Chicago, IL	Hotels, Investments
160	James Pritzker	2	55	Chicago, IL	Hotels, Investments
160	Jean (Gigi) Pritzker	2	44	Chicago, IL	Hotels, Investments
160	Jay Robert (JB) Pritzker	2	41	Evanston, IL	Hotels, Investments
160	John P Calamos & Family	2	66	Naperville, IL	Mutual Funds
204	Kenneth C Griffin	1.7	37	Chicago, IL	Hedge Funds
215	Neil Gary Bluhm	1.6	68	Chicago, IL	Real Estate
215	Nicholas J Pritzker II	1.6	62	Chicago, IL	Hotels, Investments
215	Michael Krasny	1.6	53	Highland Park, IL	CDW Corp
215	William Wrigley Jr	1.6	42	Lake Forest, IL	Chewing Gum
242	Oprah Winfrey	1.5	52	Chicago, IL	Television
322	Joseph D Mansueto	1.2	50	Chicago, IL	Morningstar
354	Marvin J Herb	1.1	69	Chicago, IL	Soft-Drink Bottling, Real Estate

400 Riches Americans – Source , From Forbes Magazine 2006

Rank	Name	Net Worth ($Bil)	Age	Residence	Source
374	John Hammond Krehbiel Jr & Family	1	68	Lake Forest, IL	Molex

Maine's Billionaires

Rank	Name	Net Worth ($Bil)	Age	Residence	Source
16	Abigail Johnson	13	44	Boston, MA	Fidelity
35	Edward Crosby Johnson III	7.5	76	Boston, MA	Fidelity
107	Amos Barr Hostetter Jr	2.6	69	Boston, MA	Cable Television
140	John E Abele	2.2	69	Boston, MA	Boston Scientific
160	Jim Davis & Family	2	63	Newton, MA	New Balance
189	Peter M Nicholas	1.9	65	Boston, MA	Boston Scientific
242	Amar Gopal Bose	1.5	76	Framingham, MA	Bose
297	Robert Kraft	1.3	65	Brookline, MA	Paper, Packaging
297	Thomas John Flatley	1.3	74	Milton, MA	Real Estate
297	Richard J Egan	1.3	70	Hopkinton, MA	EMC Corp
354	John P Manning	1.1	58	Boston, MA	Real Estate
374	Paul Barry Fireman	1	62	Brookline, MA	Reebok

Minnesota's Billionaires

Rank	Name	Net Worth ($Bil)	Age	Residence	Source
70	Richard M Schulze	3.6	65	Edina, MN	Best Buy
107	Carl Pohlad	2.6	91	Minneapolis, MN	Banking
133	Glen Taylor	2.3	65	Mankato, MN	Printing
160	Barbara Carlson Gage & Family	2	64	Minneapolis, MN	Carlson Cos.
160	Marilyn Carlson Nelson & Family	2	67	Minneapolis, MN	Carlson Cos
215	Whitney Macmillan	1.6	77	Minneapolis, MN	Inheritance
215	Cargill Macmillan Jr	1.6	79	Wayzata, MN	Inheritance

400 Riches Americans — *Source , From Forbes Magazine 2006*

Rank	Name	Net Worth ($Bil)	Age	Residence	Source
215	W Duncan Macmillan	1.6	76	Wayzata, MN	Inheritance
278	Stanley Stub Hubbard	1.4	73	St Mary's Point, MN	DIRECTV
322	William W Mcguire	1.2	58	Wayzata, MN	Insurance
374	Dwight D Opperman	1	83	Dellwood, MN	Publishing

Michigan's Billionaires

Rank	Name	Net Worth ($Bil)	Age	Residence	Source
64	William Morse Davidson	4	83	Bloomfield Hills, MI	Glass
73	Richard M Devos	3.5	80	Ada, MI	Alticor
140	Roger S Penske	2.2	69	Birmingham, MI	Cars
160	Ronda E Stryker	2	52	Kalamazoo, MI	Stryker Corp.
204	Jon Lloyd Stryker	1.7	48	Kalamazoo, MI	Stryker Corp.
242	Michael Ilitch	1.5	77	Detroit, MI	Pizza
278	A Alfred Taubman	1.4	82	Bloomfield Hills, MI	Real Estate
322	William J Pulte	1.2	74	Bloomfield Hills, MI	Home Building
354	Daniel Gilbert	1.1	44	Livonia, MI	Quicken Loans
374	John W Brown	1	72	Kalamazoo, MI	Stryker Corp.

Wisconsin's Billionaires

Rank	Name	Net Worth ($Bil)	Age	Residence	Source
45	John R Menard Jr	5.2	66	Eau Claire, WI	Home Improvement Stores
52	Herbert V Kohler & Family	4.5	67	Kohler, WI	Plumbing Fixtures
107	Kenneth Hendricks	2.6	65	Beloit, WI	Building Supplies
215	H Fisk Johnson	1.6	48	Racine, WI	SC Johnson & Sons
215	Imogene Powers Johnson	1.6	76	Racine, WI	SC Johnson & Sons

400 Riches Americans – Source , From Forbes Magazine 2006

Rank	Name	Net Worth ($Bil)	Age	Residence	Source
215	S Curtis Johnson	1.6	51	Racine, WI	SC Johnson & Sons
215	Helen Johnson-Leipold	1.6	49	Racine, WI	SC Johnson & Sons
297	Donald J Schneider	1.3	70	Green Bay, WI	Trucking
322	Robert William Galvin	1.2	84	Marshfield, WI	Motorola

Washington's Billionaires

Rank	Name	Net Worth ($Bil)	Age	Residence	Source
1	William Henry Gates III	55	50	Medina, WA	Microsoft
5	Paul Gardner Allen	16	53	Seattle, WA	Microsoft, Investments
15	Steven Anthony Ballmer	13.6	50	Bellevue, WA	Microsoft
70	Jeffrey P Bezos	3.6	42	Seattle, WA	Amazon
153	Craig O Mccaw	2.1	57	Seattle, WA	Mccaw Cellular
278	James Jannard	1.4	57	San Juan Islands, WA	Oakley
354	John Orin Edson	1.1	74	Seattle, WA	Leisure Craft
354	Howard S Schultz	1.1	53	Seattle, WA	Starbucks
374	Charles Simonyi	1	58	Medina, WA	Microsoft

Pennsylvania's Billionaires

Rank	Name	Net Worth ($Bil)	Age	Residence	Source
85	Henry Lea Hillman	3	87	Pittsburgh, PA	Industrialist
140	Mary Alice Dorrance Malone	2.2	56	Coatesville, PA	Inheritance
160	Margaret Hardy Magerko	2	40	Belle Vernon, PA	84 Lumber
160	Leonore Annenberg	2	88	Wynnewood, PA	Publishing
242	James Kim & Family	1.5	70	Bryn Mawr, PA	Microchips
322	Alfred P West Jr	1.2	63	Paoli, PA	SEI Investments
322	Richard Mellon Scaife	1.2	74	Pittsburgh, PA	Investments
354	Dorrance Hill Hamilton	1.1	78	Wayne, PA	Inheritance

400 Riches Americans − *Source , From Forbes Magazine 2006*

Ohio's Billionaires

Rank	Name	Net Worth ($Bil)	Age	Residence	Source
83	Leslie Herbert Wexner	3.1	69	Columbus, OH	Limited Brands
133	Carl Henry Lindner Jr & Family	2.3	87	Cincinnati, OH	Investments
160	Clayton Lee Mathile	2	65	Dayton, OH	Iams
242	Nancy Lerner	1.5	46	Cleveland, OH	Inheritance
242	Norma Lerner	1.5	70	Cleveland, OH	Inheritance
242	Randolph D Lerner	1.5	44	Cleveland, OH	Inheritance
297	Richard T Farmer	1.3	71	Cincinnati, OH	Cintas Corp

Connecticut's Billionaires

Rank	Name	Net Worth ($Bil)	Age	Residence	Source
67	Edward S Lampert	3.8	44	Greenwich, CT	Investments
85	Steven A Cohen	3	50	Greenwich, CT	Hedge Funds
117	Paul Tudor Jones II	2.5	52	Greenwich, CT	Hedge Funds
160	Karen Pritzker	2	48	New Haven, CT	Hotels, Investments
242	Peter Buck	1.5	75	Danbury, CT	Subway
374	Mary Anselmo	1	77	Greenwich, CT	Panamsat
374	Richard S Fuld Jr	1	60	Greenwich, CT	Lehman Brothers

Colorado's Billionaires

Rank	Name	Net Worth ($Bil)	Age	Residence	Source
31	Philip F Anschutz	7.8	66	Denver, CO	Investments
34	Charles Ergen	7.6	53	Denver, CO	EchoStar
204	John C Malone	1.7	65	Parker, CO	Cable Television
242	James Leprino	1.5	69	Denver, CO	Cheese
278	Pat A Stryker	1.4	50	Larimer, CO	Stryker Corp

400 Riches Americans – *Source , From Forbes Magazine 2006*

Rank	Name	Net Worth ($Bil)	Age	Residence	Source
322	Thomas Bailey	1.2	69	Aspen, CO	Mutual Funds
354	Gary Magness	1.1	52	Denver, CO	Cable, Investments

New Jersey's Billionaires

Rank	Name	Net Worth ($Bil)	Age	Residence	Source
21	Jacqueline Mars	10.5	67	Bedminster, NJ	Candy
38	Donald Edward Newhouse	7.3	76	Somerset County, NJ	Publishing
117	Peter R Kellogg	2.5	64	Short Hills, NJ	Investments
242	David Tepper	1.5	48	Chatham, NJ	Hedge Funds
278	Michael F Price	1.4	54	Far Hills, NJ	Investments

Missouri's Billionaires

Rank	Name	Net Worth ($Bil)	Age	Residence	Source
14	Jack Crawford Taylor & Family	13.9	84	St Louis, MO	Enterprise Rent-A-Car
107	Ann Walton Kroenke	2.6	56	Columbia, MO	Wal-Mart
140	Nancy Walton Laurie	2.2	55	Columbia, MO	Wal-Mart
153	E Stanley Kroenke	2.1	59	Columbia, MO	Sports, Real Estate
215	Pauline Macmillan Keinath	1.6	72	St Louis, MO	Inheritance

Nebraska's Billionaires

Rank	Name	Net Worth ($Bil)	Age	Residence	Source
2	Warren Edward Buffett	46	76	Omaha, NE	Berkshire Hathaway
133	J Joseph Ricketts & Family	2.3	65	Omaha, NE	TD Ameritrade

400 Riches Americans – *Source , From Forbes Magazine 2006*

Rank	Name	Net Worth ($Bil)	Age	Residence	Source
297	Walter Scott Jr	1.3	75	Omaha, NE	Construction, Telecom
354	Gary L West	1.1	60	Omaha, NE	West Corp.
354	Mary E West	1.1	60	Omaha, NE	West Corp.

Nevada's Billionaires

Rank	Name	Net Worth ($Bil)	Age	Residence	Source
3	Sheldon Adelson	20.5	73	Las Vegas, NV	Casinos, Hotels
32	Pierre M Omidyar	7.7	39	Henderson, NV	EBay
107	Stephen A Wynn	2.6	64	Las Vegas, NV	Casinos, Hotels
322	David A Duffield	1.2	66	Incline Village, NV	Peoplesoft
322	William Samuel Boyd	1.2	74	Las Vegas, NV	Casinos, Banking

Kansas' Billionaires

Rank	Name	Net Worth ($Bil)	Age	Residence	Source
19	Charles De Ganahl Koch	12	70	Wichita, KS	Oil, Commodities
140	Min H Kao	2.2	57	Mission Hills, KS	Navigation Equipment
215	Donald Joyce Hall	1.6	78	Mission Hills, KS	Hallmark
242	Gary L Burrell	1.5	69	Stilwell, KS	Navigation Equipment
278	Phillip Ruffin	1.4	70	Wichita, KS	Casinos, Real Estate

400 Riches Americans – *Source , From Forbes Magazine 2006*

Washington D. C.'s Billionaires

Rank	Name	Net Worth ($Bil)	Age	Residence	Source
107	Mitchell P Rales	2.6	50	Washington, DC	Danaher Corp
117	Steven M Rales	2.5	55	Washington, DC	Danaher Corp
242	Theodore N Lerner	1.5	80	Washington, DC	Real Estate
374	Robert L Johnson	1	60	Washington, DC	Black Entertainment Television

Virginia's Billionaires

Rank	Name	Net Worth ($Bil)	Age	Residence	Source
21	John Franklyn Mars	10.5	70	Arlington, VA	Candy
21	Forrest Edward Mars Jr	10.5	75	Mclean, VA	Candy
215	Winnie Johnson-Marquart	1.6	47	Virginia Beach, VA	SC Johnson & Sons
278	Frank Batten Sr	1.4	79	Virginia Beach, VA	Landmark

Georgia's Billionaires

Rank	Name	Net Worth ($Bil)	Age	Residence	Source
17	Anne Cox Chambers	12.6	86	Atlanta, GA	Cox Enterprises
189	Bernard Marcus	1.9	77	Atlanta, GA	Home Depot
297	Arthur M Blank	1.3	64	Atlanta, GA	Home Depot
322	S Truett Cathy	1.2	85	Atlanta, GA	Chick-Fil-A

North Carolina's Billionaires

Rank	Name	Net Worth ($Bil)	Age	Residence	Source
52	James Goodnight	4.5	63	Cary, NC	SAS Institute

400 Riches Americans – *Source , From Forbes Magazine 2006*

Rank	Name	Net Worth ($Bil)	Age	Residence	Source
117	Clemmie Dixon Spangler Jr	2.5	74	Charlotte, NC	Investments
140	John Sall	2.2	57	Cary, NC	SAS Institute
278	Ollen Bruton Smith	1.4	79	Charlotte, NC	Speedway Motorsports

Arizona's Billionaires

Rank	Name	Net Worth ($Bil)	Age	Residence	Source
153	Bennett Dorrance	2.1	57	Paradise Valley, AZ	Inheritance
297	John G Sperling	1.3	85	Phoenix, AZ	Apollo Group
297	Peter Sperling	1.3	46	Phoenix, AZ	Apollo Group
354	Arturo Moreno	1.1	60	Phoenix, AZ	Lboards

Tennessee's Billionaires

Rank	Name	Net Worth ($Bil)	Age	Residence	Source
94	Martha R Ingram & Family	2.9	71	Nashville, TN	Ingram Industries
140	Frederick Wallace Smith	2.2	62	Memphis, TN	FedEx
197	Thomas F Frist Jr & Family	1.8	68	Nashville, TN	HCA Healthcare
242	Brad M Kelley	1.5	49	Nashville, TN	Tobacco

Oklahoma's Billionaires

Rank	Name	Net Worth ($Bil)	Age	Residence	Source
27	George B Kaiser	8.5	64	Tulsa, OK	Oil & Gas, Banking
215	Tom L Ward	1.6	47	Edmond, OK	Chesapeake Energy
215	Aubrey K Mcclendon	1.6	47	Oklahoma City, OK	Oil

400 Riches Americans — *Source , From Forbes Magazine 2006*

Rank	Name	Net Worth ($Bil)	Age	Residence	Source
242	David Green	1.5	64	Oklahoma City, OK	Hobby Lobby

Maryland's Billionaires

Rank	Name	Net Worth ($Bil)	Age	Residence	Source
197	Bernard Francis Saul II	1.8	74	Chevy Chase, MD	Banking, Real Estate
197	Richard Edwin Marriott	1.8	67	Potomac, MD	Hotels
204	John Willard Marriott Jr	1.7	74	Potomac, MD	Hotels
354	Stephen J Bisciotti	1.1	46	Millersville, MD	Outsourcing, Football

Indiana's Billioniares

Rank	Name	Net Worth ($Bil)	Age	Residence	Source
80	William Alfred Cook	3.2	75	Bloomington, IN	Medical Devices
107	Melvin Simon	2.6	79	Indianapolis, IN	Real Estate
278	Dean V White	1.4	83	Crown Point, IN	Lboards, Hotels
322	Herbert Simon	1.2	71	Indianapolis, IN	Real Estate

Arkansas' Billionaires

Rank	Name	Net Worth ($Bil)	Age	Residence	Source
6	Jim C Walton	15.7	58	Bentonville, AR	Wal-Mart
7	S Robson Walton	15.6	62	Bentonville, AR	Wal-Mart
11	Helen R Walton	15.3	86	Bentonville, AR	Wal-Mart

400 Riches Americans – *Source , From Forbes Magazine 2006*

Idaho's Billionaires

Rank	Name	Net Worth ($Bil)	Age	Residence	Source
59	Robert Earl Holding	4.2	79	Sun Valley, ID	Energy, Resorts, Ranching
80	John Richard Simplot & Family	3.2	97	Boise, ID	Potatoes, Microchips

Utah's Billionaires

Rank	Name	Net Worth ($Bil)	Age	Residence	Source
57	James L Sorenson	4.3	85	Salt Lake City, UT	Medical Devices, Real Estate
242	Jon Meade Huntsman	1.5	69	Salt Lake City, UT	Chemicals

Other's

Rank	Name	Net Worth ($Bil)	Age	Residence	Source

Oregon's Billionaire

Rank	Name	Net Worth ($Bil)	Age	Residence	Source
30	Philip H Knight	7.9	68	Beaverton, OR	Nike

Alabama's Billionaire

Rank	Name	Net Worth ($Bil)	Age	Residence	Source
242	Marguerite Harbert	1.5	83	Birmingham, AL	Inheritance

Montana's Billionaires

Rank	Name	Net Worth ($Bil)	Age	Residence	Source
98	Dennis Washington	2.8	72	Missoula, MT	Construction, Mining, Transportation
160	Linda Pritzker	2	52	St Ignatius, MT	Hotels, Investments

400 Riches Americans – *Source , From Forbes Magazine 2006*

Rank	Name	Net Worth ($Bil)	Age	Residence	Source
South Dakota's Billionaire					
117	**T Denny Sanford**	2.5	70	Sioux Falls, SD	Banking, Credit Cards
South Carolina's Billionaire					
354	**Jerry Zucker**	1.1	57	Charleston, SC	Industrialist
New Hampshire's Billionaire					
85	**Patrick Joseph Mcgovern**	3	69	Hollis, NH	IDG
Wyoming's Billionaire					
7	**Christy Walton & Family**	15.6	51	Jackson, WY	Wal-Mart Inheritance
Louisiana's Billionaire					
215	**Phyllis Miller Taylor**	1.6	65	New Orleans, LA	Taylor Energy
Road Island's Billionaire					
297	**Hope Hill Van Beuren**	1.3	72	Middletown, RI	Inheritance
Hawaii's Billionaire					
17	**Barbara Cox Anthony**	12.6	83	Honolulu, HI	Cox Enterprises

400 Riches Americans – *Source , From Forbes Magazine 2006*

American Billionaire citizens living in other countries

Rank	Name	Net Worth ($Bil)	Age	Residence	Source
98	Barbara Piasecka Johnson	2.8	69	Monte Carlo, Monaco	Inheritance
140	Evgeny (Eugene) Markovich Shvidler	2.2	42	London, United Kingdom	Millhouse Capital
197	J Russell Deleon	1.8	40	Gibraltar	Online Gaming
197	Ruth Parasol	1.8	39	Gibraltar	Online Gaming
204	Ernest E Stempel	1.7	90	Haton, Bermuda	Insurance
215	Marion Macmillan Pictet	1.6	74	Haton, Bermuda	Inheritance
215	Victor Fung	1.6	61	Hong Kong	Distribution
242	Marc David Rich	1.5	71	Meggen, Switzerland	Commodities
322	William E Connor II	1.2	56	Hong Kong	Supply-Chain Services
322	Pincus Green	1.2	71	Meggen, Switzerland	Commodities
374	Louis Moore Bacon	1	50	London, United Kingdom	Hedge Funds
374	Robert M Friedland	1	56	Singapore	Mining

The Wise Rich Man

Scriptural References:

Proverbs 19:17 He that hath pity upon the poor lendeth unto the LORD; and that which he hath given will he pay him again.

Genesis 1:28 And God blessed them, and God said unto them, Be fruitful, and multiply, and replenish the earth, and subdue it: and have dominion over the fish of the sea, and over the fowl of the air, and over every living thing that moveth upon the earth.

Genesis 9:1 And God blessed Noah and his sons, and said unto them, Be fruitful, and multiply, and replenish the earth.

Genesis 22:18 And in thy seed shall all the nations of the earth be blessed; because thou hast obeyed my voice.

Genesis 24:1 And Abraham was old, and well stricken in age: and the LORD had blessed Abraham in all things.

The Wisdom of Solomon
Ecclesiastes 9:11

I returned, and saw under the sun, that the race is not to the swift, nor the battle to the strong, neither yet bread to the wise, nor yet riches to men of understanding, nor yet favour to men of skill; but time and chance happeneth to them all.

PASTOR THORNTON BELL, SR.

Pastor Bell was saved in 1982, sanctified, and filled with the Holy Ghost at the Seed of Abraham Pentecostal Church in Renton, Washington - a suburb of Seattle. He and his wife, Pastor Shelia Bell, are co-workers in the Gospel of Jesus the Christ. Although they have ministered together in Mexico, London, Manchester, and Kenya and Zimbabwe, Africa, and were ordained Pastors in Denver, Colorado, they both are currently working to save, heal, and set the captives free in Birmingham, Alabama in the name of Jesus the Christ and our Lord. God is blessing them, and they are giving God the glory.

www.ingramcontent.com/pod-product-compliance
Lightning Source LLC
Chambersburg PA
CBHW032020090426
42741CB00006B/673